Lost Civilizations

Investigations Into the Lost Civilizations of Lemuria

(The Enigmatic Disappearance of Ancient Civilizations That Still Mystify)

Angela Valdez

Published By **Simon Dough**

Angela Valdez

Lost Civilizations: Investigations Into the Lost Civilizations of Lemuria (The Enigmatic Disappearance of Ancient Civilizations That Still Mystify)

ISBN 978-1-77485-691-8

Legal & Disclaimer

The information contained in this ebook is not designed to replace or take the place of any form of medicine or professional medical advice. The information in this ebook has been provided for educational & entertainment purposes only.

The information contained in this book has been compiled from sources deemed reliable, and it is accurate to the best of the Author's knowledge; however, the Author cannot guarantee its accuracy and validity and cannot be held liable for any errors or omissions. Changes are periodically made to this book. You must consult your doctor or get professional medical advice before using any of the suggested remedies, techniques, or information in this book.

Upon using the information contained in this book, you agree to hold harmless the Author from and against any damages, costs, and expenses, including any legal fees potentially resulting from the application of any of the information provided by this guide. This disclaimer applies to any damages or injury caused by the use and application, whether directly or indirectly, of any advice or information presented, whether for breach of contract, tort, negligence, personal injury, criminal intent, or under any other cause of action.

You agree to accept all risks of using the information presented inside this book. You need to consult a professional medical practitioner in order to ensure you are both able and healthy enough to participate in this program.

TABLE OF CONTENTS

Introduction 1

Chapter 1: The Minoans (2000-1400 Bce) 5

Chapter 2: The Maya (250-1697 Ce) 43

Chapter 3: Lost Cities 69

Chapter 4: The Maya 83

Chapter 5: The Indus Valley Civilization . 89

Chapter 6: Angkor 94

Chapter 7: How Do We Have A Clear Understanding Of Our History? 109

Chapter 8: Enigmatic Easter Island 146

Conclusion 183

Introduction

It's been my pleasure to present you with book that cover a variety of ancient civilizations. From the mystery of Egypt to the strength of the military of Rome and from the philosophy from the Greeks to the mythologies of the Norse we've traveled across the globe to uncover the mythologies, beliefs, and ways of life of our ancient time.

The most fascinating aspects of the past, archaeology and anthropology isn't always discovered. The majority of the world's civilisations have disappeared or have evolved so dramatically that their historical roots are virtually gone to antiquity. We're talking, of course about the ancient civilizations of the world.

By forgotten civilizations, I'm certainly not talking about myths, or theorized civilizations such as Atlantis. Instead I'm talking about the people and cultures that are known to exist and left behind clues to their origins.

There's a lot to learn about the history of humanity however, there are plenty of questions. In general, it appears to be the greater we learn it's the greater number of questions that we are asked.

The book we'll explore these ancient civilizations which passed through the centuries with traces of their ancient cultures. From the ancestral Pueblo Culture in North America to the Khmer Empire in Asia and beyond, we'll explore the fascinating people of these cultures and what we know about them and the legacy they left in their wake.

This book isn't a comprehensive study of every lost civilization the globe has ever encountered. There are many lost civilizations and peoples that we have a good idea of and, I would think, a lot of them that aren't known about so that a comprehensive study is a sloppy picture. It has been a pleasure for me to create this book to provide readers with information about a variety of the world's most intriguing lost civilizations.

To limit the contents of this book on the most relevant and pertinent civilizations certain conditions were enacted. The first and most important thing is that every civilization within this group has left behind some kind of evidence to prove its existence. There are numerous theories of societies that were debated on a particular level or other throughout time, with no tangible evidence of their existence, such civilizations can't be studied with any degree of scientific accuracy or veracity. In addition there are other civilisations (like those in Punt in Africa perhaps stretching into in the Arabian Peninsula) which are mentioned by different groups, however there are no archaeological sites or artifacts related to the said civilization has yet been discovered.

The second reason is that while the most attention has been given to those civilizations that have left us with an idea of its as well as its character and culture, there are a few sites that are captivating enough to not miss. In these instances there is as much evidence and theories as is possible is included in order that you, as the reader, will be able to better understand, using your own thoughts what these ancient civilizations might have been about.

The third option is given to those that are representative of a total civilization that is either gone or has changed its nature in such a way that its historical roots do not play any significance in its current character.

This is to give the most complete information in a single glance, but still allowing space for as many civilizations as are possible. The section for each civilization will usually contain a brief introduction and a review of what they left behind and interesting information or theories that are based on findings of the remnants of the civilization and culminating with an explanation of how the civilization ended. While some of these societies like the Maya for instance left enough evidence to fill a volume, other civilizations that merit an investigation have left tiny. This book serves as a general overview of the civilizations in this book and not as an exhaustive examination of only a few of these fascinating civilizations.

Thanks again, I hope you enjoy it!

Chapter 1: The Minoans (2000-1400 Bce)

Minoan is the name that was coined. Minoan is actually the creation of an archaeologist called Sir Arthur Evans. In the beginning of the 20th century Evans visited the location in Knossos (which we'll talk about more in a second) and when he saw them thought he had discovered, completely the royal palace known as Minos. This is the reason why the ancient civilization was found on the island of Crete.

Although it is possible it is the case that the Minoan Civilization actually began, in any form or fashion way earlier and ended later than previous period, it was the time period 2000-400 BCE when The Minoan Civilization thrived.

What do they have left to be left behind?

The Minoans left a lot to Crete. Crete with their artifacts that are found all over the region. The most interesting discoveries, however, are those of Phaistos, Zakros, Malia and, in particular, Knossos.

As with many other ancient civilizations, Minoans left behind a vast quantity of pottery of various kinds, with different ways of function and form. They also created a couple of alphabets that are yet to be figured out such as the hieroglyphic alphabet and the one called Linear-A.

Interesting facts

The Minoans were by necessity, a sea-based culture. This can be derived from the evidence of their trade relations with other cultures and peoples that are influenced by different cultures, for instance, the influence of the Egyptians on Minoan art, and to a lesser extent architecture and Minoan products that were found in other countries.

The Minoans are famous for, however, is their architectural remnants. Within the Minoan cities, there are numerous burial chambers, domiciles and, in each of them, there are also enormous palace complexes that housed trade, religious practices and political/administrative functions. These palaces are several levels high and cover many thousands to thousands of square feet.

In the Greek mythology of the Minotaur the king Minos (for who they, along with the Minoans and, naturally the Minotaur in itself were named) that was believed to have built the labyrinth where the evil Minotaur lived. This legend is explored in depth by a separate book in this series called Discovering Ancient Greece.

Minoans were also one of the first civilisations to Europe to have water running and roads with paved surfaces.

What happened to the Minoans?

It's not clear what caused the Minoan civilization waned There exist a variety of theories.

Another theory is Mycenaeans took over the Minoans on Crete. Crete but this would suggest that the Minoans existed significantly longer than the time period 2000-400 BCE. It isn't possible but. One could be presented that the Minoans even though their influence and culture diminished, they continued to exist as a group up until the point they either assimilated or took into the hands of Mycenaeans.

Another theory that has lots of evidence to support it is that around fifty years before the dramatic decline in Minoan society it was the time of a major volcanic eruption that was located about sixty miles away from Crete. The theory is minoans were afflicted terribly due to this natural disaster as well as the subsequent tsunamis and earthquakes that caused the disaster in the islands.

We'll never know for sure what exactly happened and how or when Minoan Civilization fell, but with the Palace of Knossos and other structures and artifacts that they left in their wake, we're unlikely to forget them anytime in the near future.

The Mycenaeans (1600/1450-1200 BCE)

The Mycenaeans are frequently referred to by the name of "the early Greeks" due to the fact that they were the ones who were the first to speak the Greek language. But they weren't, in fact the first inhabitants of what would later become Greece. Much like the Minoans prior to them The Mycenaeans were a part of the locations in the Greek island Crete and, similar to the Minoans who preceded them, the Mycenaeans would be brought to an abrupt conclusion.

Responsible for a lot of architecture and art along with religion and trade that had a significant influence on the region in both their period and after. Mycenaeans were often a tough and severe culture.

It was in Mycenae who wrote the poem of Greek epics, the Iliad as well as The Odyssey, Homer, wrote King Agamemnon as a ruler who was from and in the city the area where the forces who were to invade Troy at the time of the Trojan Wars originated.

What were they able to leave in their wake?

It is believed that the Mycenaeans leave behind variety of items that would later be used to influence how we see the future for Greece. Perhaps most importantly, and it's difficult to say that the Mycenaeans developed Linear B, a language which, although it was inspired by Minoans' Linear A language, could be a model for the language used by later Greeks inside and beyond the island of Crete. Contrary to Linears A as well as C Linear B has been discovered and, because of this, we now know more concerning the workings and inner workings Mycenaeans that we have in the majority of Minoans.

In addition to the written language, Mycenaeans left behind a huge quantity of weapons, pottery paintings/frescoes/murals, jewelry and even architecture. A majority of Mycenaean cities were constructed with huge palaces that although they varied in certain aspects based on the location and location, shared many elements that would continue in the direction of Greek architecture for decades to come. The most notable of these is that of Megarons. Megarons. Megarons were the main focal element of the Mycenaean palaces, and were made by three distinct features including an entrance as well as an antechamber, and finally the hall itself. The hall was the place that the chief of an Mycenaean city could have their chambers of the throne.

The most well-known Mycenaean centers which I'm sure I'm belief that you'll recognize these cities which were Mycenae, Athens, Sparta and Thebes. With their expertise in trade and overall prosperity the cities would thrive as trade centers that brought in wealth of precious metals, jewels as well as spices and other important items. Mycenae however was the main center of this group in the period.

One of the most fascinating remains of those of the Mycenaeans is the large hive-shaped burial chambers where they laid to rest their royalty as well as other nobles. The tombs were covered with artificial mounds, which meant they were mostly underground. Inside, they were spacious and circular with ceilings that were domed and reach a point at the top, hence generating the nickname "Beehive Tombs."

Interesting facts

The Mycenaeans were heavily influenced by their Minoan predecessors. There are some similarities in religious symbols, but it's not clear whether they utilized these objects to continue Minoan Beliefs or the Minoan Belief system in itself or as a means to show their gratitude and respect for the Minoans. Some of the items that are discovered in the Mycenaean and Minoan civilisations are figures and designs of double-bladed knives.

The Mycenaeans As mentioned earlier were skilled traders and prolific and their products have been discovered in areas such as Mesopotamia, Egypt, Sicily and Anatolia. Together with oil (olive not petroleum) as well as other food items and other food items, the Mycenaeans traded precious stones and metals like copper, ivory and gold. They were also famous for their expertise in the art of making glass.

What did happen with the Mycenaeans?

It isn't confirmed with certainty. There was a time when it was widely believed that the Mycenaeans were defeated by Doric attacks from north Greece but it is now up for debate. However, it is probable that during the demise of the Mycenaeans that there were numerous conflicts or, at most, there was a lot of turmoil within the community since numerous Mycenaean sites were destroyed or otherwise destroyed throughout this time. Actually, it's the idea of internal conflict which seems to have gained the most support in this debate because it seems like the gap in wealth increased beyond control. This type of wealth accumulation is a long-standing one of the main reasons in the demise of many of the greatest civilizations but most especially the one of Rome and Rome, since it tends to weaken the general economy, production of goods , and the morale of the majority of the population.

There is a hypothesis that a prolonged drought resulted in an earlier Mycenaean civilization to fall away but this theory is now being discredited more and more because of the absence of evidence supporting this kind of event in the time of this event.

Olmec Olmec (1200-400 BCE)

Our journey begins by looking at the Olmec which is generally considered to be the most complex civilization in Mesoamerica1. Its name Olmec (orig. Olmecatl of the Aztec) roughly translate to "rubber individuals." The name was coined by the Aztec to describe the Olmec's method of extracting and using rubber, particularly latex, from trees.

They lived in the area that is today Mexico.

What were they able to leave in their wake?

The Olmec left behind several sites, including San Lorenzo, Laguna de los Cerros, La Venta and Tres Zapotes in modern-day Mexico. In these sites are located the earliest evidence of Mesoamerican pyramids, which are also known as step-pyramids due to their construction. In addition to these structures one of the most intriguing things the Olmec left behind was 17 heads made of stone, probably showing Olmec leaders.

There are also a few examples from the Olmec language that is a written form with glyphs that is possibly one of the oldest Mesoamerican language for which we know of.

Interesting facts

Olmec Olmec were traders, and they built an extensive civilization from this method. They were a hierarchical community however the precise social structure is a bit difficult to determine from current excavations. We are discovering every day more information about Olmec but, the excavations continue.

The Olmec featured intricate and impressive architecture and art. Alongside the massive statues they also made statuettes and embellished their structures with a elegant, artistic style.

They also played playing a game with a rubber ball commonly referred to"the ball game. "the ball game." They were the first to introduce this game, although other civilizations later adopted the game. There isn't much information about the guidelines of this game however, one variant was played only with hips. The goal as archaeologists and other anthropologists have been capable of determining was to move the ball to the opposing team's goal zone. These games were probably quite brutal, given that depictions of them often include players wearing protective gear and evidence suggests that in certain versions of the game (specifically in the case of the Aztecs however, it is likely to be played among Olmec and other tribes,) the losing team was likely to be executed. It is believed that players who won a game will gain some sort of status or social standing.

What did happen to the Olmec?

The Olmec did not completely die off after its end civilisation's power. A large portion of their cities were abandoned before the evident "fall" of the Olmec however, some of their cities were very well-populated. The main reason behind the decline of the Olmec was its integration with other groups nearby. Olmec influence is evident across a variety of Mesoamerican civilizations, even after the demise of the Olmec civilization itself, however it is not as evident that the spread of Olmec statues and other artistic influences would fade away in the year 400 BCE. There is a belief people that Olmec are the ancestral and the ancestors of the Mayans but this idea isn't yet proven.

The Chavin (900-200 BCE)

One of the first cultures of South America, the Chavin took their name from the location that was Chavin de Huantar which is an ancient temple remains near the Andes in the northwest of Peru.

There is a belief that the Chavin were the most likely to be the first large and diverse community in the region to embrace one religion and, perhaps, a political structure however, the latter isn't sure.

What do they have left to be left behind?

In Chavin de Huantar, a large and intricately decorated temple complex was discovered. The temple was made of four-sided stone and featured sculptures on the walls as well as the pillars.

They also left behind pottery such as decorative jugs, which include, among others

17

depicted crocodiles as well as other reptiles such as cats, birds, and even human beings. These designs can also be seen in various forms of art like crowns, sculptures, steles masks, and jewelry.

Interesting facts

One of the most powerful people in the Chavin culture were priests, or shamans. With the purported authority of God they could influence people in any direction they decided to take. It was through the religion that people gained control, and it was through their faith that they ruled the masses. They had no claim to authority. All their authority was derived the belief system.

The Chavin mixed a range of symbols from the culture and religion of other people and used these concepts to form their own faith. The result was a stunning impact as the display of these new blended symbols and beliefs were presented in a manner that they appeared old-fashioned.

There were a variety of methods used in rituals to place the participants and/or shamans to shame in the spotlight, such as ritual sacrifice as well as the use of hallucinogenic drug and coca, as and bloodletting.

What did happen to the Chavin?

It's difficult to know exactly what led to the demise of Chavin culture. It is believed that some communities continued to exist in the area after the fall of Chavin. It is possible that once united peoples fell under political or civil conflicts that were that were too big to resolve and then warred or broke up, but it's speculation.

The Nabataeans (312 BCE-105/106 CE)

The Nabataeans are among the most obscure groups listed on this list. Their roots are unknown to antiquity. dates of the 312 BCE below is not the first reference that is known to the Nabataeans which is an Arabic people which was mentioned in a report from the Third War of the Diadochi. In the time of this report they were Nabataeans existed as a thriving civilization that was able to fight in the face of Greek forces, and it's likely that their culture existed for a while prior to the publication of this account.

However, the Nabataeans are frequently referenced in mythological terms in the mythologies and histories that were prevalent at the time. Although there is much to be learned about the history of the Nabataeans and their culture, there are some of the most important aspects of their civilization (at least for a time following 312 BCE) as well as if the Nabataeans who we recognize as historical are the same as those mentioned in mythologies of different groups, there's an enormous amount of curiosity about these peoples. And they've left us with some truly amazing examples of their nature.

What do they have left in their wake?

While the Nabataeans left some of their marks in the form of statues, pottery and metalwork. Most known remnants from the Nabataeans is their architectural style. Of these, the most notable are those that are located in Avdat, Shivta (though there is a growing trend that suggests Shivta as the site of a Byzantine agricultural settlement , not an actual Nabataean city) and the remarkable Capital city, Petra2.

Avdat is situated in Israel it is a city destroyed by time that was a major stopping point for the Nabataeans in their journey to Petra because it was a major point along the trade in spices and incense route that connected Petra as well as Gaza. It is most well-known to visitors of today for its Acropolis. The city would later be taken over by different peoples: It was inhabited by Romans and Byzantines. However when Nabataea was annexed by Roman Emperor Trajan It is possible that while Romans and Byzantines could also be able to live in this city however, it was the Nabataeans were still there, only changing their names as Nabataean citizen in to Roman and Byzantine citizens or citizens. The city would eventually be destroyed and cease exist during the seventh century because of the massive damage caused due to an earthquake.

It's with Petra however the true splendor of the Nabataeans can be discovered. Petra can be described as a town located in an area of desert, with a lot of it built within the limestone cliffs that make up contemporary Jordan however, it's not a cave-like home. The architectural style is a strong evidence in Greek influence, but Petra's character is its own. Although there has been many civilizations that lived on and around cliffs however, the size and the quality of the Nabataean structures within Petra is unique.

It's not all of Petra is included in these architectural masterpieces However. Within the cliffs lie a portion of the town, structures as well as other significant regions, many of which are still used to a certain extent or in another way by Bedouin people. Petra was the heart of Nabataea and was home to large numbers of traders, travellers and was home to an estimated number of 30,000. Virtual tours of Petra accessible online, so even in the event that you don't plan to visit Jordan but you're still able to take a glimpse of Petra, one of the more captivating and fascinating cities in the history of the world.

Interesting facts

Even though both the Nabataeans as well as the Romans could eventually coexist well, they were at one time on opposite sides of the battlefield. Julius Caesar had been assassinated and Parthian forces tried to take advantage of the situation, observing Roman colonies in Jordan as available amid the chaos, though only for a short period because Augustus was soon to become the Emperor and the Nabataeans were eventually allied with the Parthian forces. Rome however was awe-inspiring in its army, and the Parthian as well as Nabataean forces would soon surrender to Rome. It didn't end Nabataea in any way but it did result in an extremely difficult situation for them. It was due to the Roman demand that Nabataeans pay homage to Rome. This was made even more difficult by the fact that the Nabataeans were in a position of being unable (perhaps not willing?) for payment of the Roman tribute in a couple of instances prompting a quick and brutal response from Rome's Roman military. The wars of the era that Rome defeated portions of Nabataea and also certain trade routes that ran to the north.

It was with Rome where the destiny of Nabataea was to be tied to from that point on however, this wasn't always a totally antagonistic relationship.

What did happen what happened to the Nabataeans?
The Nabataeans were not completely dispersed or exiled from their homelands, however, they were to become Romans.

At the time of 70 CE In the year 70 CE, the Nabataeans, despite earlier battles with Rome were able to join the Roman forces in the suppression of an uprising of Jewish inhabitants of Rome. Although this might have temporarily made relations between Rome and the Nabataeans better however, Rome had its eye at Petra and the declining but still profitable trading routes used by the Nabataeans.

The whole thing would culminate during the time of Rabbel II Soter (Soter which means "savior of all the inhabitants") the final King of the Nabataeans. There are a few versions of what happened. claim Rabbell II Soter as the king. Rabbell II Soter made a agreement with

Rome in which, as that as long as Romans did not leave Nabataea at peace during the time King Rabbell II Soter (King Rabbell II Soter) lived and reigned, the Nabataeans were not going to fight the Roman the encroachment of Nabataea following his death.

It is unclear if this agreement was concluded according to these reports or not it is clear that it is clear that the Roman Emperor Trajan did in fact invade Nabataea just after Rabbell's death. Rabbell and was able to withstand virtually no opposition like he did. This is how Nabataea was incorporated into Rome.

Nazca Nazca (200 BCE to 600 CE)

The Nazca were named after the region where they thrived. Like the earlier civilizations they Nazca resided in the region that is currently Peru. Their most famous cities are known as Ventilla or Cahuachi.

What do they have left to be left behind?

The most striking and distinctive remains from the Nazca are the massive geoglyphs they compiled. They were essentially art of such an extent that they are best seen from the skies. They are also referred to in The Nazca Lines.

The geoglyphs vary in subject matter from animals like monkeys and birds, to images of people , or in some cases, plain lines. The Nazca Lines have captured the interest of almost every person who has encountered them or seen images and videos. The exact reason for their creation is unclear, however they're certainly one of the most intriguing things to be invented.

Alongside the Nazca Lines and the Nazca Lines, the Nazca people also made multicolored pottery. It was made using an handle that was that was placed between two spouts over the glass jug.

At Ventilla at Ventilla, the Nazca built aqueducts under the sea to safeguard their irrigation water from the sands of Nazca Desert. Ventilla was the political and social capital in the Nazca. In Cahuachi the center of spirituality of the Nazca is a little over three dozen mounds connected through the central plaza. The celebrations of religion were celebrated in Cahuachi and this can be deduced from numerous examples of broken pottery, which were likely used for catering to celebrations and feasts.

Interesting facts

The Nazca people did not have the rule of a central government. Rather every region was split into distinct political centers. Think of it as the state governments of each. Although the Nazca did collaborate to help difficult areas, and for other reasons but there was not a one governing body that covered each of the areas.

The Nazca also utilized metalworking to serve practical purposes and also for artistic and decorative reasons.

What happened to Nazca?

The Nazca were their own worst enemies. Through the years of clearing, cutting, and gathering lumber, they knowingly removed their new areas of agriculture without protection from the erosional forces. Particularly useful in this area to ensure stability and fertility to the soil , is the Huarango species with deep roots that are capable of lasting for around 1000 years. The huarango tree survived in the desert due to the deep roots that could not only collect subterranean water for its personal usage, but also brought water up to be used for the neighboring plants. Once these forests vanished and a huge El Nino came in in the year 500 CE, their culture was already in decline. In the absence of a way to shield your fields against the devastation they had created, Nazca collapsed.

Moche (1-800 CE) Moche (1-800 CE)

It is believed that the Moche were a population that were widely distributed in modern-day Peru even before the Inca became famous. Although they are often referred to as the Moche are often thought of as a single group, however, with distinct differences in art, architecture and two distinct languages most likely what we call"the" Moche were two distinct allied groups.

What were they able to leave in their wake?

The majority of what was discovered of the Moche earlier, especially in the 80s, was location of their city of the identical name. Its city Moche has revealed two knolls with pyramidal forms, commonly known as The Temple of the Sun and the Temple of the Moon, which were constructed from brick and workshop houses, homes storage facilities, plazas and houses as well as other architectural treasures.

In addition to these architectural relics as well as these architectural elements, the Moche were talented craftsmen and artists. In addition to decorative images of a variety of shapes, usually of heads or jaguars reclining on top of the vessel. They also had a knack for metal, and a variety of necklaces, headdresses and other jewelry types were found.

Since the 1980s, numerous additional Moche places have been discovered and many contain pyramids, despite the fact that lots of looting has occurred through the centuries.

Interesting facts

The Moche as well as other civilizations previously mentioned in the past, was a cult of sacrifice for human life. In actual fact, the remains of approximately forty young men were discovered at the foot of the Temple of the Moon.

The Moche had irrigation canals and were skilled in regards to agriculture. They had numerous villages and cities, many of which were administered by distinct rulers, similar to local governors.

Numerous tombs and burial grounds have been found and provide us with an understanding of the stratification of social status in moche culture. Moche culture. The most affluent would typically be buried with expensive jewelry in semi-private or private burial sites, while the more commoners were typically confined to less grand final resting places.

What was the fate of the Moche?

The exact date is not certain. In the 8th century, the civilisation began to decline rapidly. It's possible they migrated or were hit by natural catastrophes, such as earthquakes, drought or floods. There is also the possibility that shifting sand might cause their towns to become inhabitable. We have evidence of canals being flooded with sand dunes from the nearby area prior to the decline of the civilization itself.

"The Aksum Kingdom/Empire (100-940 CE)

It is believed that the Aksum (alternately Axum) were people from Ethiopia that, although believed to have come from Sabaean immigrants, grew out of indigenous populations in the area. At one time Aksum was a vast empire. Aksum Empire was vast, that extended from present-day Ethiopia up to Yemen, Saudi Arabia, Eritrea and Sudan.
Although it's possible that Aksum existed in some form or the other long before the advent of the common era it was at the start in the 2nd century of CE when it began to develop and take over the entire region.

What were they able to leave to be left behind?

Aksum Aksum left behind cities like Aksum, Matara, Adulis, Yeha and Qohalto, in addition to others. In addition they left a number of burial grounds/cemeteries, stelae as well as other cultural and architectural artifacts from these cities.

The biggest single-stone obelisk of the world is located in Aksum. This stone was created to pay tribute to the life of a presumed wealthy and powerful person however, it is likely that when the five-hundred-ton, one-hundred-foot-high Obelisk was being raised it fell, falling onto the tomb that was originally created from the earth to honor (how's irony?) It is here that it sits among the many other (and significantly smaller) Obelisks.

One of the most striking obelisks provides a glimpse of an of the more powerful ruling families from the Aksumites. It's The Ezana Stone which documents the hardships of the Aksum King called Ezana (ruled from 320 to 360 CE.) The stone tells a tale in three languages (Sabaean Ge'ez, Shabaean, as well as Greek) regarding the monarch's defeat of the other six rulers.

The background of Ezana is fascinating because when he started his rule as a pagan, it was his first Christian Aksum King. This would bring about one of the first Christian nations. Aksum was one of the first countries in the world to have an image of Christianity as the symbol on its currency Some of which is still in use.

Interesting facts

One of the most interesting aspects of the story attributed to Aksum is the fact that they believed it to be the final resting location for the Ark of the Covenant. Although this object has obviously, not been discovered however, it gives an idea about the concept of the kingdom prior to the change to Christianity and was believed to be the ideal spot for an artifact of this kind to rest. Aksum is also believed to be the final place of residence for queen of Sheba mentioned within the Hebrew Bible and the Qur'an as possibly being one of King Solomon's love interests and speculated to be the queen, or at the very least among the females that rhapsodized on within the Biblical book called the Song of Solomon.

The Aksumites were thought to be among the main world powers of the time, alongside Rome, China and Persia and their influence can be seen across the world in the past when they traded all over the world and conquered a variety of nations.

It was a rich society, however like most civilizations throughout time, the inequality of wealth was a lot and the Aksumites had a system of feudalism with regards to agriculture, and also held slaves.

What has happened with the Aksumites?
A number of forces were involved in the demise of Aksum although it's unclear which of them helped end the empire as it was.

The theory that is most popular is that Aksumite Empire was defeated or at the very minimum significantly weakened due to foreign invasions by either the Jewish queen known as Yodit although her existence is highly debated or Damoti, a pagan queen.

Both are traditional, local histories that are not likely, but it is well-known that the Aksumite Empire was frequently in the crosshairs of outsiders just as every other major civilization in time was. These attacks by a multitude of groups of outsiders eventually forced Aksum to consolidate and cause the Aksumites to consolidate and weaken their empires on an massive size. So, regardless of whether any of these queens actually existed, or even if they existed have anything to do with the decline of Aksum or not, it does provide some perspective to the Aksum mentality both in the past and in more recent.

What is certain is that another group that resided within Aksum known as"the Agau (alternately Agew or Agaw) gradually gained power, and eventually overthrew the traditional Aksumite rule to make way for its own dynasty, called the Zagwe. After this shift in the leadership and the Zagwe's leadership, the Aksumite Empire would be gone however the land would be in the hands of people.

It is the Ancestral Pueblo Culture (100-1600 CE)

The long-running name of the Navajo term Anasazi The Ancestral Pueblo Culture was one of the most important Native American tribes in what is today in the United States. Although their roots are obscure to the time of antiquity We do have the evidence for at least seven times in that Ancestral Pueblo Culture timeline: the Second Basketmaker period and the Third Basketmaker period and the First Second, Third Fourth, Fifth3 Pueblo times.

The immediate descendents of the Anasazi who were given the name of by the Ancestral Pueblo Culture by the Navajo meaning, "Ancestors of the Enemy," would go on to form several Pueblo tribes, including the Acoma The Hopi of as well as the Laguna as well as the Zuni tribes.

They primarily lived in the the present-day "four corners" area in the United States. This is where the boundaries of four of the U.S.

States Utah, Colorado, Arizona and New Mexico meet.

What were they able to leave to be left behind?

Ancestral Pueblo Culture began. Ancestral Pueblo Culture began and in a certain degree it would remain in pithouses4, caves and recesses inside valleys, mountainsides mesas, hillsides and valleys. The other structures included pits for food storage that were covered to avoid infestation and to encourage the preservation of food. A lot of these structures remain in operation today.

In addition numerous carvings ceramics, milling stones, ceramics,, and other tools, as well as baskets and flutes too.

Interesting facts

Prehistory from that of the Ancestral Pueblo Culture is broken into six distinct periods, mostly for anthropological and archaeological convenience. What exactly transpired in these periods is only known from the artifacts left from various times.

It is possible that you be aware that the initial period is referred to as"The Second Basketmaker Period.. There was once a time known as"the First Basketmaker Period, but more research has revealed that the traits believed to be common in the now defunct division of Prehistory from the ancestral Pueblo Culture typifies the Second Basketmaker Period. Instead of getting rid of the Third of these times and moving the remaining ones back by a few years, to ensure continuity, archaeologists as well as Anthropologists have preserved the names of different periods as they are.

In this article, we'll look at an in-depth look at the characteristics that was typical of these prehistoric periods.

The Second Basketmaker Period is known by its name for the use and design of beautifully constructed baskets. At this time it was believed that it was believed that the Ancestral Pueblo Culture were hunters and gatherers, even though they were also cultivating maize or corn.

The Third Basketmaker Period saw greater agricultural activities and the introduction of irrigation within the group which included the building of reservoirs and dams. The first domesticated animals were introduced to eat and the number of animals was growing rapidly during this time. Although hunting and gathering was common, it wasn't relied on as much as it was in second Basketmaker Period.

The First Pueblo Period saw the development of above-ground dwellings typically consisting of huge connected structures, which included numerous dwellings, as well as others, such as the ones for religious ceremonies. These ceremonial chambers, also known as Kivas were made of round stones and were dug into the ground. The use of masonry/stonework started to become more popular and widespread.

It was the Second Pueblo Period was noted for the significant expansion of pottery and other hand-crafted crafts however also the variety and design of the Ancestral Pueblo Culture settlements. Kivas also witnessed a kind of revival, which is now being constructed in larger shapes and usually within taller structures instead of being solely underground.

The Third Pueblo Period is when the most famous and striking settlements were built: the settlements built on cliffs. The settlements of these times were typically large. While some contained only few dozen dwellings and private spaces, some were larger and contained up to 1,000 rooms. In this period the art that was characteristic of Ancestral Pueblo Culture reached its highest point and, even though smaller settlements were mostly abandoned however, the Ancestral Pueblos enjoyed a time of stability.

The stability would come to an end however, in this Fourth Pueblo Period. With droughts-- specifically the great drought between 1276 and 1300--causing irreparable damage to agriculture, making the Ancestral Pueblo way of life very difficult to maintain. The Ancestral Pueblo were moving, and even building larger and more extensive settlements. But, due to their wars between those of the Apache and Navajo and the loss of a lot of their agriculture and the Ancestral Pueblo tradition was severely diminished.

What changed with What happened to Ancestral Pueblo Culture?

In 1598 CE (incidentally the year that marked the beginning of the modern , or fifth Pueblo Period,) the Spanish began to settle in what is today what is now the United States, and sought to introduce Christianity (usually with guns) to native tribes. Although there was an uprising at the end of 1680 CE among people from the Ancestral Pueblo and various tribes, their freedom didn't last for long.

At the start of the 1700s CE, with the constant snares and assaults by those of the Spanish and other colonial forces as well as the diseases spread by European invaders and in the Ancestral Pueblo Civilization had been much weakened. However their descendants from the peoples of this time live on although much of their tradition has gone away or changed (though certain groups continue to adhere to their traditional customs) and their first settlements have been abandoned.

Chapter 2: The Maya (250-1697 Ce)

The first thing to note is that the above beginning time of the Mayan civilization demands some clarification. The initial Mayan cities were built between 200 and 250 CE and would be the beginning of what's known as the Classic Period of the Maya but the Mayans themselves had existed as a more loose agricultural community. It is believed that the first settlements that could be traced back to the Mayans were established around 1500 BCE. Their civilization gradually growing in complexity towards 200 CE.

There were around 40 cities in their peak The major Mayan cities included Tikal, Bonampak, Uaxactun, Dos Pilas, Calakmul, Copan and Palenque. It is estimated that in the most prosperous period, the Mayan civilization had about 2,000,000 inhabitants and more than 2 dozen Mayan languages remain in use, to an extent, even today. They primarily resided in the area of the southern part of Mexico and in the northern part of Central America, extending into areas of the modern-day

Guatemala, Honduras, El Salvador, Belize and the Yucatan Peninsula.

What were they able to leave to be left behind?

Maya Maya left us with a lot of amount of evidence and, in actual they were still around in the years before (and up to) they were destroyed by the Spanish Conquistadors arrived in the sixteenth century BCE. There are still cities that contain Mayan step-pyramids , art particularly carvings and statues and terraces that were utilized to facilitate some of their more advanced farming methods, balls courts, and the most famously, their clever calendar system. They also had their own language of glyphs that has been mostly, but not entirely, deciphered. This has revealed much more about their society, including their beliefs and the societal structures.
Interesting facts

The Mayans were extremely mathematicians and astronomers. Their religion was tightly tied to their observations of the astronomical world. This society and religion were not as peaceful as was once believed However, deeper knowledge of Mayan glyphs has revealed the fact that a civilization often waged combat with rival cities, or even the other Mayan city, while even human sacrifice, and the torture of captives was not unheard of.

In particular, over the past few years, a more intense curiosity about this particular Mayan Calendar has arisen with many people believing there was some chance that our world was likely to shift or end and/or that Mayans themselves believed that this would be the case, since they believed that the Mayan Calendar "ran out" or, more precisely it only went into 2012 CE. (Yeah this is where the idea originated.) Although this has earned some people lots amount of cash, you can observe, the world is still in existence and is generally similar to it was prior to 2012. What is the Mayan Calendar or, more precisely, calendars , is notable is the extremely precise forecasts of eclipses as well as other astronomical phenomena, such as astonishingly precise predictions for the position for Venus as well as the moon.

The Maya also utilized the number zero as a math principle which was actually not present generally among the civilizations of the past. We have taken for granted the "number" zero as a given nowadays but in the past it was a important thing, and surely contributed to the incredible accuracy of their calculations.

What is the fate of the Maya?

The Mayan civilization was declining significantly at the time of 900 CE mostly due to the effects of drought and changing climates. However there were traces from the ancient civilization which included those that are still inhabited, but still distinct Mayan cities, remained till the Spanish Conquistadors massacred the majority members of the Maya and then seized the Mayans remaining cities. In the years that followed, the majority people Mayans had left their urban centers and were returning to a rural community of small settlements centered around their primary agriculture areas. A lot of Maya who did manage to survive the ferocious assault of conquistadors were taken captive and sold to slavery.

Maya Maya even despite myths are still a people in the present, with they still adhere to certain aspects of their culture but now it's generally incorporated into Christian practices.

Khmer Empire Khmer Empire (802-1431 CE)

It is believed that the Khmer Empire was the civilization which arose from to the present-day Cambodia however, it also extended into areas of Laos, Vietnam and Thailand. It was most famously recognized for its religious tradition that was a mixture of Buddhism as well as Hindu (depending on the period and location) with the most famous remains was Angkor Wat: Quite probably the biggest religious complex witnessed anywhere in the world.

What were they able to leave in their wake?

The Khmer were extremely skilled builders who built a variety of huge structures, primarily for worship services, however, they also had structures for political as well as civilian uses. Angkor Wat is the largest of these, covering 200 acres (492 acres) and was also a Hindu temple, although it later became an important Buddhist sacred site.

Angkor Wat is often referred to as the eighth wonder of the universe and, while other tourist destinations are also identified with this name, it surely offers a huge advantage over its counterparts. If you have the chance, I'd strongly recommend taking a trip to Angkor Wat. It truly is an incredible and amazing buildings anywhere in the world.

Interesting facts

The Khmer loved celebrating their holidays. There were a myriad of events, including horse races dancing, fireworks, dances as well as cockfights and other music festivals There was every day something to celebrate in Khmer.

For the Khmer they weren't always excitement and games. In the course of the empire and throughout its history, the Khmer battled and (usually) stopped fights and revolts from within and outside. Many nobles who were dissatisfied with their large fortunes could begin an revolt against Khmer to gain their own fame. Unfortunately, this is something we've witnessed throughout history and continues to witness today. Internal disputes were common as the succession to throne following the death of a king was frequently questioned.

Under the reign of Jayavarman VII (1181-1218 CE,) the Khmer would remove an occupying force in the capital city Angkor of a group known as the Chams. The Chams weren't just exiled by the ruler, however, Jayavarman VII would then go into battle with Champa in the city (home to Chams.) Cham population.) In this time that the Khmer areas would expand to the greatest extent and a large portion of the structure of the Khmer would be constructed by Jayavarman VII, who commissioned a variety of churches, monuments, hospitals, and most importantly, Angkor Thom which, unlike Angkor Wat which was a temple, was built to be a city in that city called Angkor.

What has happened to the Khmer?

Khmer Empire Khmer Empire was eventually overrun by the people of Thailand who fled Mongol attacks. There were Thai settlements being built for a few years but it was not until the Mongols started to fight with greater force within China and the surrounding areas it that the largest portion of the migration took place. The Thai started to build their own cities, and as their cities grew more filled with people and became more strong The Thai began to attack Khmer cities and regions and eventually led to the demise of the Khmer Empire which was at this point, in financial distress and suffering due to the constant internal turmoil of its leadership.

Toltec (900-1100 CE). Toltec (900-1100 CE)

The Toltec were among the more militaristic communities that existed in Latin America. The exact date or manner in which the Toltec were formed is not known, however they appeared on the scene with fervor when they attacked their city Teotihuacan around 900 CE. The Toltec are generally believed to have been a part of the same group in some way, at the very least in large part for about a century prior to this time.

It is located in Teotihuacan is often regarded as belonging to Toltec construction, though this is speculation. It will be explored more in the Aztec section of this chapter.

You'll be surprised by the fact that it was long the belief it was believed that it was the Toltec are a mythological civilisation and that the beliefs, artifacts and beliefs. were in fact invented by groups that came in prominence afterward, including the Aztecs. The theory has been widely dismissed because, in the wake of discoveries in Toltec archaeological sites as well as the comprehensive understanding of the Toltec handed down by the Aztecs There is no doubt about the truth that the Toltec.

What do they have left in their wake?

Much of the finer things in the Toltec's collection were stolen at one point or other time, excavations have provided many insights to the Toltec capital city, Tula or Tollan.

Tollan, also known as the City of Reeds, is usually believed to be close to a modern city of the identical name. In this area, excavations have revealed an ancient Toltec city which could have housed hundreds of thousands of inhabitants. In this area, there is a massive plaza or mall at the heart in the center of town. On one side there is a pyramid made of five huge steps. Steps here refer to the design, not stairs that people could climb however, the pyramid does have steps also. The pyramid, like other structures that are part of the area thought to be Tollan however in lesser amounts are decorated with different decorations including carvings, sculptures and paintings of human heads that protrude out of the mouths of cats, serpents and dogs, as well as an escalator that led up to a two-roomed section in the middle.

Together with two other pyramids in this city's zone, there are a variety of carvings, statues, an estate for the palace and two courts to play ball.

Although other Toltec sites are not as well-known however, they are there in some extent and can give us an understanding of the history that was the Toltec. Additional information is passed down at first by the Aztecs who believed or knew they were descendents of the Toltec who they considered to be highly respected.

Interesting facts

Mixcoatl Theorized as The Toltec leader who commanded the destruction of Teotihuacan might have actually brought the Toltec on the map however it was Ce Acatl, his son Topiltzin Quetzalcoatl who would establish the Toltec ways of life and even, as it is believed to have modified and accelerated the reverence for the serpent with feathers. In the Toltec religion, this god was referred to as Quetzalcoatl

While there were many other religions5 in those of the Toltec, the legend of the serpent with feathers Quetzalcoatl left an impression on subsequent civilizations, especially Maya and Aztec. Aztec as well as the Maya.

They Toltec were also famous craftsmen, who were extremely skilled in the construction of statues, Chac Mool statues6

What is the fate of the Toltec?

A loose group of different people, known as Chichimec. Chichimec or Chichimeca was invaded by the north. The Chichimec group was comprised of various tribes, including the Aztecs, who are believed as having conquered tollan, the capital of Tollan.

It is not known much about the other tribes that were part of these peoples however it is believed that they were at some point in the past, or at a later time, nomadic. The Aztecs became the dominant power among the invading tribes in the 15th and 16th centuries.

The Aztecs (1100-1521 CE)

The Aztecs were at first part of a number of northern invaders referred to in the Chichimec. Although this group began its move around in the same period, it is seen as an influx of different tribes rather than a strict alliance.

As Tenochtitlan would later become the Aztec capital prior to the building of the city, the Aztecs were from north, and had settled on islands within Lake Texcoco.

What were they able to leave in their wake?

Tenochtitlan is Tenochtitlan, the Aztec capital, was actually founded as a settlement that spanned two islands in Lake Texcoco. The current capital of Mexico, Mexico City, is located on the same spot as Tenochtitlan. Tenochtitlan could eventually expand to encompass five square miles. This included areas on artificial islands.

When the conquistadors came to the region they estimated that the inhabitants in Tenochtitlan to be in the vicinity of 400 000 people. Tenochtitlan was the home of temples as well as vast markets which are estimated to have 60,000 people daily would be involved in some form of trade. Similar to other people within the region, Aztecs also played ball as well as courts were discovered in Tenochtitlan.

The Aztec left many pieces of information, including their techniques for agriculture, herbs medicine and their language (still used today, and by the people who descend from the Aztecs as well as others from and in central Mexico) in addition, for those who might say, in a playful way chocolate.

Along with these contributions, the Aztecs also left structures--including pyramids--and carvings, statues and mythology. The statue of Montezuma (alternately, Moctezuma,) was discovered.

Interesting facts

The Aztec civilization was so rapid and was stable due to their extensive utilization of agriculture. The Aztecs did not only Aztec establish irrigation for their crops that were spread across every square inch of land and not used in any other way They also managed to restore land that was once wetlands or swamps.

The present Mexican flag is decorated with an eagle sucking snake. This image comes drawn from an Aztec legendthat tells of the story of how Tenochtitlan became a settled city. It is believed that Huitzilopochtli the name of Huitzilopochtli means blue Hummingbird from the South predicted that the Aztecs would locate their homes when they saw an adulterated eagle that was eating a snake sitting on the plant called a cactus. After a long search and a long wait, the sight was observed on an island in Lake Texcoco. As the later Aztec generation believed was the place of their seat of power.

Similar to other civilizations of this region, Aztecs also had the Aztec calendar. They were similar to those of the Maya as well as other Mesoamerican groups in that it comprised of a 260-day ritual year, which was synchronized with a calendar that was 365 days long.

Aztecs Aztecs were also famous for their practices that involved human sacrifice. While other groups practiced this practice in different degrees but the Aztecs are believed to be the most prolific when it comes to its usage. A popular method of offering sacrifice for the Aztec was to remove and following offering of the heart of the deceased to Tonatiuh tonatiuh, the Aztec god who was the Sun's protector. There were there were other methods of sacrifice, such as skinning, bloodletting, dismemberment and decapitation are also used but it is also possible that these stories have been exaggerated, or, in certain instances in some cases, invented through the Spanish Conquistadors to justify for their massacre of Aztec.

In addition to worshiping other gods like Quetzalcoatl and the feathered serpent and Tlaloc the god of rains The Aztec believed in the earth to be just one in the creations and was the only one of its kind. According to Aztec beliefsystem, Earth was covered by 13 distinct worlds, including nine beneathworlds.

What has happened in the Aztec?

Simply put, Cortes and his merry group of murderous conquistadors were killed. The events are well-documented.

The Spanish arrived in Tenochtitlan around 1519 CE. Cortes was a distinct kind of wild savages. Cortes was at first chosen by the Governor of Cuba and upon which the Spanish established numerous settlements, in order to discover more peoples and cities that could offer the same kind of gold and treasure that the Spanish had extracted from the corpses from the Mayans.

But, when Cortes began to build a military that was larger than the governor expected, or was at ease with, the governor tried to summon Cortes. Cortes's brother-in-law, as a demonstration of the blood-sucking nature of the conquistadors killed the envoy, who carried the papers that relieved Cortes from his control. Knowing the governor's disapproval Cortes did not bother to read the writ only to delay his departure.

After arriving at the shore, Cortes originally made camp with the Totonac people however, before long an ambassador from Aztec was sent by Montezuma. In a regal attire, the messenger was presented with a demonstration of the weapons and troops of Cortes and returned to Montezuma to be given more instructions on how he would prefer to proceed.

After hearing of the strength of the Spanish Montezuma was worried that Cortes was actually, Quetzalcoatl, returning to claim his kingdom. In the meantime, Cortes, unable to return to Cuba since he could likely be executed for his disobedience to the governor, made the settlement. In order to stop those who were committed to Spain from leaving, he burned his own vessels.

When Cortes took his troops towards Tenochtitlan they encountered an armed group called the Tlaxcalans. The Tlaxcalans initially fought Cortes however, they were beaten by Spanish forces, they finally made peace to Cortes and joined his battle to eradicate the Aztec culture that he was yet to see.

While on his way, Cortes, his men and the newly-drafted Tlaxcalans killed a group known as the Cholulans. The massacre sparked fear in the region and several groups just complied with what Cortes wanted.

When he reached Tenochtitlan The king of Tenochtitlan, Montezuma, attempted to calm the bloodthirsty Spaniard by gifting him with presents which included a necklace composed of precious gold and stones. Cortes, in true fashion did not hesitate to return the gesture, however, the necklace that he bestowed on Montezuma was largely out of cut-glass.

Tensions were at a high. The Aztecs knew about Cortes's reputation. Cortes was a tyrant. This was the time Cortes locked up Montezuma for the purpose of controlling his will through Montezuma.

The Aztecs began to rebel. They were no longer confident in Montezuma because the Aztecs believed that he was too in love with the pale beast. Cortes began to demolish Aztec idols, and then substituting them with images and idols of Christianity.

The governor had sent an arrest team following Cortes and his men, Cortes, with a surprise attack defeated the arrestersand enlisted the dead to bolster his own military forces. Alvarado who was the man Cortes removed from the helm of Tenochtitlan when he was killing his potential arresters, saw many of the Aztec nobles killed.

After Cortes's return and his re-election, Montezuma was forced to try to end the animosity between the Aztecs however, Montezuma was repelled, being hit with rocks and shot with bows. In the meantime it was clear that Aztecs were in the process of destroying the city. Aztecs were destroying or taken away causeways and bridges leading to Tenochtitlan along with the Spanish were at risk of revenge. In view of Montezuma as having no more use, since his people refused to follow him Cortes killed the once-great Emperor and the Aztecs and began killing many of the nobility.

When news of Montezuma's death was spread and spread, the Aztec people were finally fed up enough Cortes. The conquistador as well as his men tried to escape but were discovered to be Aztecs who killed anywhere from 600 to 1,000 Spanish. Estimates put the number of killed Tlaxcalans in the hundreds of thousands.

Although the Aztecs believed that they had driven out the Spanish forever, Cortes employed the unique geographical location in Tenochtitlan in his favor and unleashed smallpox on the Aztecs. Soon the Aztec empire was reduced to Tenochtitln itself. With its population divided hungry and dying of the biological war Cortes unleashed upon them the last defense of the Aztecs was destroyed.

Inca Inca (1200-1532 CE)

It's odd to think this one of the famous lost civilizations of our time was so short in timeline. If you consider the period prior to recorded history in the past, the Incans were a relatively young group. However, they had an intriguing culture that continues to be relevant even to this day.

In this short time The Inca were extremely powerful and, by the time they had finished their culture their influence spread across all along the Pacific Coast of South America starting from central Chile all the way to the north-western boundary of present-day Ecuador. The majority of this expansion occurred in a period of thirty years between 1463 and 1493.

The Incan people probably existed prior to 1200 CE however it was at this time that they consolidated and more of a power across the continent.

What do they have left to be left behind?

The Inca left behind a treasure-trove of pottery and ceramics even though the majority of their precious metals, including gold, were taken and then melted to make use for the Spanish Conquistadors in the 17th century, some remains.

It is believed that the Incan capital city was Cuzco but, possibly most well-known among these Incan cities Machu Picchu. The Incans are well-known for their architecture which is particularly apparent when you visit Machu Picchu. The city is situated on top of a high mountain (literally,) between two mountain peaks.

Machu Picchu is generally believed to be Palace of Pachacuti Inca Yupanqui, emperor of the Incans between 1438 and 1471 CE. Even though Cuzco is widely believed to be the best stonework in the world, Machu Picchu is particularly amazing due to its location and numerous features including stone steps, terraces and the cemetery. Additionally, Machu Picchu is the site of The Temple of the Sun.

Cuzco can also be of special importance because the temples are made of stones that are so thin that knives cannot get in the spaces between the massive stones. In contrast to Machu Picchu, which was abandoned many centuries years ago Cusco has a population of more than 300,000 people in the present.

Similar to those of North as well as Central America, the Incans also constructed step pyramids. Many of these structures and other architectural wonders remain standing.

Interesting facts

The Incas were mathematicians who were also Astronomers. Although they were unable to anticipate eclipses like other Central American peoples, they were able to identify solstices and equinoxes. it was through their knowledge of astrology that they formulated their calendar. The calendar was lunar which is, one that was based on the cycles of the moon, from Full moon through full moon, or perhaps, from the new moon to the new moon. They could not do this without writing a language.

Pachacuti Inca Yupanqui, referenced in the previous section, came to power through the use of his brother. This is the first date that archaeologists can affirmatively put in the Incan timeline: It was 1432 in the year. While the Incans were certainly present prior to this date no specifics are discovered prior to this date.

At this time during this period, the Incans took over many countries expanding the borders of their empire in the direction of the northern and southern. In the final days of the emperor who succeeded him, Topa Inca Yupanqui (ruled 1471-1493 CE) in 1471, the

Incan Empire was reaching its greatest expanding to its south.

The Incan Empire can be described to be an oligarchic empire. The Emperor was the highest in the scale, but most of the wealthiest of citizens also assisted the Emperor during his reign. The law was strictly enforced. The Incans were adamant about animal and human sacrifices in their religion.

The Incans created numerous routes throughout the empire and this helped their trade and military expeditions. Farmers, the Inca created and traded many kinds of food items, goods and livestock.

One of the most infamous of the Incan products was coca that is one of the plants from which cocaine made. Coca leaves were typically chewed, and were often utilized to increase productivity, even though it was also seen as the majority of its usage in rituals and in medical.

The Incans are famously known for performing a type of brain surgery, but this name is a bit confusing. It's true that the

Incans were the first to develop, and eventually were quite proficient in the method of drilling into the skull to treat head injuries which was typically sustained during combat. The 15th century was the time when it was estimated that 90percent of the operations were successful and patients went into the next century after the procedure.

What was the fate of the Inca?

Like the other civilizations mentioned in the previous chapter The Incan civilization came to an end when it was rediscovered by the Spanish Conquistador. The conquistador was christened Francisco Pizarro.

While Pizarro could be the final blow the resurgence of rivalries between two brothers who were proclaiming lordship over Inca contributed to the process of their demise. In addition there was the fact that the Incas had been in encounters with Europeans and thus fell in the path of diseases that did not exist previously in the region and that the Incas were unable to fight.

Chapter 3: Lost Cities

We've explored a variety of lostancient civilizations but there are some archaeological discoveries that are a little smaller, but generally smaller, or less impressive, size. These are just a few examples of the most lost (and discovered) cities in the world.

Although different civilizations have occupied diverse parts of the world in different periods but they all share the rich human history, often challenging the conventional wisdom and providing more detail to the human history.

Troy (3000/2920 BCE-1100 CE)

It was long believed to be the work from Homer as well as his fellow comrades due to the fantastical stories of The Iliad as well as the Odyssey The site of the ancient city of Troy is now known. Although the majority of the stuff Homer describes about the city as well as the time period in his epics can be often dismissed as untrue however, there is a rich story behind the city, making Troy one of the more intriguing archeological sites around the globe.

Troy was found in the Hissarlik mound in present-day Turkey which was where it had been for many years buried and has provided us with an abundance of information about its history. Much like Troy, which was the Troy in the works of Homer and Herodotus the town of Troy was surrounded by walls of defense and a couple of dozen parts have been unearthed. This, in addition to 10 gates and around fifty strongholds show the story that Troy was heavily focused on defense. This is a good thing, since Troy was repeatedly attacked and overwhelmed.

A lot of the background of Troy is not known or ambiguous because a large part of what we know about it was influenced by the beliefs of the religions at the period. We do know that Troy fell several times throughout its time of existence. It is interesting that after Troy was devastated whether it was by intruders or natural disasters like earthquakes, the people living in Troy did not completely clear of the debris, but instead constructed a new version of Troy on top of the debris.

There are a variety of archaeological finds and structures found during the excavations from 1865 to 1868 comprise objects like jewelry and coins from monuments, theaters, and stones that bear Greek writing as well as defensive structures, and a variety of structures like the concert hall, market and council house. The distinctive way Troy was constructed on the remains of its own has provided us with a better understanding of the city's history across different times (nine nineteen years, to be precise.)

In the past, Troy was a great intermediary between Anatolia, Troas, the Black Sea and the Aegean Sea as well as the Balkans and the surrounding regions. Through immigration and trade in addition to being a prominent source of information in the past, Troy would serve to connect people of different origins as well as ethnic and religious groups.

Troy was to be abandoned but would be rebuilt and then taken over by Rome and rebuilt it in the reign of Caesar Augustus. At the time it was over, the city was renamed Ilion as well as Ilium.

The end of Troy's story was less dramatic than the events of its history or the mythology surrounding it in the stories of Herodotus. Although it was devastated, destroyed, and abandoned (for different periods of time, including at one time nearly four hundred years) before being rebuilt in 700 BC damaged and rebuilt numerous times, it was to come to an end due to the decline of trade and migration, only to disappear completely at around 1100 CE.

Sanxingdui (1,600? BCE)

There is not much information about the civilization that produced the relics that were found in Sanxingdui (trans. Three Stars Mound.) Relics of a civilisation that were previously undiscovered by archaeologists were first discovered in the year 1986 . Near Guanghan in the Sichuan Province in China, the site was a sacrificial pit which contained a variety of artifacts comprising a variety made of bronze, jade, ivory, and the clamshells.

Some of these were weapons, including bronze and jade daggers and swords, decorations depicting dragons and tigers, dishesware and other items such as cups, bases for utensils, and so on.

The total yield from the first site that was the sacrificial pit totaled more than 400 individual pieces.

As excavations were coming to an end at the site, another one site was discovered just 15 miles from the site. There, bronze sculptures of animal faces were discovered as well as numerous elephant tusks and bronze objects such as jade objects, tree branches as well as a bronze statue that was cut into two pieces on different sections of the site.

As time passed it was revealed that there were more of this group of people, including canal systems, some of which seemed to be especially focused on controlling floods, and city walls that actually contained the portion that was the Mamu River, a tributary to the Yazi close to where Sanxingdui was constructed.

The Sanxingdui date is believed to fall within the time of the Shang Dynasty (1,600-1,046 BCE,) however, there aren't any documents from the past that describe the particular culture. Unfortunately, there is any writing discovered on the Sanxingdui sites to provide a glimpse of the larger society which produced these amazing artifacts. They were definitely advanced compared to their time and had developed the technique of casting bronze different from similar to that used by the Chinese people in their time in the Shang Dynasty.

There are several various theories about what happened to cause the demise of the Sanxingdui civilization It's possible that they were invading or otherwise taken over by a different group. In addition on the sites of excavation the evidence suggests the presence of a massive flooding, which could resulted in the movement or even the demise that was the Sanxingdui.

The art of these objects and the culture that created them are truly remarkable It is our hope that time and ongoing research will reveal more about the history of the society that created these treasures from Sanxingdui.

Baiae (178 BCE - 1500 CE)

Were you dissatisfied to learn that Atlantis isn't included in the book? Here's the most important (possibly superior) thing.

Baiae (also known as Baia) was an Roman city named after the helmsman of Ulysses, Baios, and was an active center of commerce. It was annexed in Caesar Augustus, Baiae was popularly referred to as a resort city for Romans because of the presence of hot volcanic springs where Romans and those who lived in Baiae prior to Augustus would bathe and relax.

Baiae even though it was commonly regarded in its time, to be an resort town, was to be involved in a wide range of problems. In addition to its eventual demise due to malaria and later submersion into the Bay of Naples, Baiae was taken over by Saracens during the 700s CE.

You might be thinking about the reason Baiae is one of the Roman city is mentioned in this book as Rome is not in the general characteristics of other civilizations in this book. In addition to being abandoned about 1500 CE due to an outbreak of malaria due to its distinctive geography and in a way, because the people who once flocked to Baiae the bay close to the city's site would eventually become Baiae while the entire city gradually sinks due to the volcanic fumes that were present in the area.

Baiae is a real sunken city that we do not just know existed, but also have discovered and can now visit. In the ruins and remains in the sunken city you will find buildings that were once bathrooms (the Romans loved their bathhouses.) They are massive, magnificent structures that were previously thought as temples. They are often referred to as by their false names, "The Temple of Mercury" or of Diana and so on.

The most striking to me, is the incredible well-preserved statues that are now adorning the shores in the Bay of Naples. It's truly surreal to gaze upon these incredible artworks, which are now submerged.

It is possible to visit the remains of Baiae via a few options such as glass-bottomed boat tours available for hire, and the site can be explored by snorkeling or scuba diving.

Great Zimbabwe (800-1450 CE)

Great Zimbabwe was a city that was home to between 17,000 and 8,000 people. It also served as a royal palace as well as the capital. It was built by the ancestors of the Shona people and situated near Masvingo, Zimbabwe, the around 1,800 acres area was home of three distinct kinds of constructions: The Hill Complex, the Great Enclosure and the Valley Complex. Each of them was utilized extensively at different times however it was possible to have some commonality, with that of the Hill Complex being the oldest (800-1200 CE), the Great Enclosure being in the middle of the period (1200-1400 CE) and the Valley Complex being the most modern (1300-1450 CE).

The remains of the city are still visible and, even while they're only less than their former splendor They still create an awe and amazement. The most famous artifacts discovered from Great Zimbabwe are a collection of eight sculptures referred to as The Zimbabwe Birds. These birds were carved from soapstone, and are typically perched on columns that were about four feet high. The birds themselves are approximately 18 inches tall.

An important center of trade during the past, Great Zimbabwe's trade reaches extended a vast distance, with artefacts found from places that range from the local region to Arabia and up to China. The majority of the products produced to be traded with Great Zimbabwe appears to be ivory, and more specifically gold. Gold was mined extensively by people from Great Zimbabwe and, for the duration of time, this made it one of the most lucrative trade centers in the region.

Similar to many of the civilizations and cities that are mentioned in this book there are many theories to explain the decline of Great Zimbabwe including such divergent possibilities as famine/drought, and protests and political turmoil about mining that led to the exhaustion of gold as well as the decline in trade because of the growth of other groups from the north.

Unfortunately, even though Great Zimbabwe is now a UNESCO World Heritage site, in the past, petty theft by enthusiasts has resulted in the most destruction to the ruin that are Great Zimbabwe. We hope that this petty crime is stopped to ensure that these magnificent ruins will last for many generations to in the future.

Shangdu (1263-1369 CE)

The infamous place of Kublai Kahn's Kahn dynasty. Shangdu is often referred to as Xanadu was built to serve to serve as the capital city of the Kahn. While Kublai Kahn would later relocate his capital to the present-day Beijing, Shangdu would serve as a base from where the Kahn would unite a variety of agricultural groups across China. This is how Kublai Kahn would ascend to the top.

Although Kublai Kahn is Mongolian however his empire, called the Yuan Dynasty, would eventually be spread across northern China and eventually become more Chinese in appearance as time passed. There was a significant mix of different cultures within Shangdu and this will create a unique place.

When Shangdu was discovered the city was filled with artifacts that were mostly comprised of construction materials, architectural remains and so on. The discovery, however, was not to last for long, and the ruins are all that is left.

In Shangdu it was a city with an inside with a palace as well as an outer city connected by canals. The city was constructed in accordance with principles and tenets of Feng Shui, Shangdu was the home of various cultures that frequently settled in different parts within the city. The thing that might be shocking to some is the fact that whenever Kublai Kahn and his Yuan Dynasty were able to conquer a certain number of individuals, they usually took great care to not let the conquered people to continue their traditional ways similar to the way that Rome did following the conquer of Greece and Greece, but their Yuan Dynasty would even go further to integrate themselves into a new tradition. This resulted in better relations with those who had been conquered but these relationships weren't universal and definitely were not sustainable.

In his time, Kublai Kahn would entertain people from other cultures including Marco Polo, the famed Spanish traveler who brought items, spices, and customs (including the use in the form of money made from paper) upon his return from a long stay in the Kublai Kahn's court. Kublai Kahn. Contrary to popular belief, Marco Polo wasn't the first European to visit and interact with the inhabitants in East Asia. Actually, Marco Polo got his beginning as a "wayfarer" (his term) business when he followed his father's journey to China following the passing of his mother. to death.

Shangdu was even home to what's known as "the big debate" that pitted those who adhered to Taoism against followers who practiced Tibetan Buddhism, and it was through this debate that Buddhism was introduced to China as well as the vast expanses across Northeast Asia.

While there is a lot to be said about the willingness to accept diversity in Shangdu, the Kahns were notoriously brutal leaders and by their regaining power the enemy, they created many enemies. In 1369 Shangdu was sacked by Ming Army. Ming Army.

In the past, Shangdu was home to around 100,000 people even though nothing aside from the remains of the once great Mongolian capital (later the capital city of summer,) the history and the wonder of Shangdu continues to be remembered.

Chapter 4: The Maya

This civilisation, which flourished for more than three (3) millennia was more popularly referred to as the prognostication civilization. Actually because of a misunderstanding of their notion of time and calendars people believed that there would be a reversal of the clock as the clock began to tick 2012.

The Location

The Empire was a part of all of the lowlands in Central America, which will place it within the Yucatan Peninsula, if it continued to thrive in the present. To have a better idea of the location of the Mayans could be if their empire were still alive There would not be Guatemala as well as Belize. A portion in Belize and the Mexican state that comprise Tabasco and Chiapas and Western areas of Honduras and El Salvador would be part of the Mayan Empire. There's a lot of territory to get your head around.

The People

Mayan People Mayan People were nature-centric. That means that their lives revolved around the seasons and cycles of nature. They were devoted to their elders and cherished their deceased.

Cultural Contribution

The Mayans were a sophisticated civilization that refined many aspects of writing, mathematics astronomy and the calendar which was developed in the region around 800 CE under the Olmecs. The Mayans wrote and used symbolism, which was written in hieroglyphics.

Beliefs and Religion

When their civilization grew, and their religion grew, so did their culture. They worshipped the Great Mother Goddess as well as a Plumed Serpent (Kukulkan) the latter being her companion. They believed that nothing ever born or dies, which was the basis for their gods as well as the way they viewed the universe.

The idea of the afterlife is derived directly from The Tree of Life, which includes thirteen levels or tiers. All are different levels of ascension.

Technology, Architecture, and Design

The most well-known structures that the Mayans are famous for are the pyramids that you are able to visit in the area. There are numerous pyramids in their society that are comprised of thirteen levels that mirror their beliefs and faith. They also constructed step-stretchways, however the focus of all structures was astronomy as well as their opinions.

What was the cause?

We are now getting to the point. What was the cause that caused a widespread culture and people to vanish?

Overpopulation

This is a more plausible theory that a lot of people are agreeing on, which is the fact that they grew out of their territory and had to relocate, however other theories were posited that was in agreement in a way with this theory.

Invading cultures

Although they weren't harmed too significantly by intruders from their oceans, they were required to fight off other cultures that were within their boundaries. This resulted in frequent border disputes, which ended in conflict or talks that included the wedding of their wives to the new culture. Many have speculated that this has caused an "watering in" of the Mayans in general and forced them to leave their communities without any explanation about what transpired.

The same goes for invaders from far away

There are some who think that the demise of these structures is due to the constant assaults by invaders from outside such as the Spaniards, the Spanish and others but, in actual the region they lived in was not a place with anything to offer the invaders. The Spaniards were seeking valuable metals, but the Mayans were left with only obsidian and limestone, which is useless to invaders who just see them as glass and rocks. The region they lived in also provided them with jade and salt as well which is something that most invaders wouldn't even know was a stone.

Remember, at the time that the Spaniards arrived at what was then known as the Mayan Empire it was already becoming a victim of nature around it. This would have prevented invasions from far.

There is a theory that it was an evaporation

There are some, with no solid evidence, who claim that a prolonged drought could have wiped out the Mayan people because water was limited for agriculture, cooking or drinking, however there is no evidence of this at present.

My Two Cents

I think there are two possible motives for the Mayan people to have to leave their cities.

Population growth, the primary reason one, may have forced them to locate an alternative area to continue their expansion. You can still see Mayans living in the area today.

Another is the influx of people from surrounding cultures that led to decades of war, border conflicts as well as the integration of their people with different cultures. The thinning of the Mayans took place in this way their society was eventually destroyed because of the death and other beliefs that led into people of the Mayan population not believed that that their ruler was divine and this was what happened. There have been many instances of civilizations being affected by external influences, and I can't think there is any reason why this shouldn't be the reason that this could have occurred.

In the case of drought, they were in a region of rain forests and, with their technological and knowledge of science they would have devised an approach to conserve the water they used during dry times.

You're the next

What did you think has happened?

What theories do you think are feasible and what is the reason?

What theories do you consider as weak and why?

Chapter 5: The Indus Valley Civilization

From the Yucatan From the Yucatan Middle East, we're going examine who the inhabitants of the Indus Valley were, and what transpired to them. There is evidence that suggests that this civilization began at around 5500 BCE.

The Location

The Indus Valley civilization were alive in the present, it would have encompassed the Northwest portion of India as well as parts from Pakistan, Iran, and Afghanistan. At its height it could have claimed nearly 10 percent of human population of the ancient world.

The People

This Indus Valley tells the story of two cities that thrived which were Moheno-Daro as well as Harappa. They were extremely developed in their civilisation, with structures , which we will explore in a different section. They were well-organized.

Cultural Contribution

The Indus Valley had a written system that is still to be decoded. Another indication of a growing and established society is arrangement of towns and cities, amulets, jewelry, pottery as well as carved seals of stamps archeologists also discovered the weight system employed as well as copper tablets.

Beliefs and Religion

Similar to similar to Mayans and the Mayans, their religion was based on nature. They believed in an ethereal Mother Goddess and God the Father God. They believed in the Tree of Life and also revered fertility symbols. They also believed in the rituals, charms and amulets as part of their magical rituals.

Architecture and Technology

They had cities that were well-developed that had multi-level homes with paved roads, underground plumbing, and functional bathrooms. They also employed metalurgical techniques.

What has happened?

In the 1800s BCE this flourishing culture started to decline. Craftsmanship and writing slowly decreased and eventually, they removed their tax system of weight and taxes. In the absence of many concrete proofs There is no evidence about the reason why they vanished however, here are some theories.

Environmental Factors

There is speculation of a dramatic drop in the amount of rain that caused drought and driving people to leave the valley. Others suggest there was an earthquake that destroyed the area.

Invaders?

Some believe that the migration of the Aryans across the Hindu Kush Mountains pushed out the culture and settled at the Indus Valley.

My Two Cents

While there might be a valid argument for the migrants who invaded, I usually find myself influenced by environmental causes. A drought could have rendered it difficult to maintain their lifestyle or cause them to die from starvation or to move to more fertile areas to live on.

It's Your Turn

What are your thoughts about what was the cause?

What theories do you think that you can believe in and what is the reason?

What theories do you think are weak? as weak and why?

Easter Island

A part of one of the more renowned or famous civilizations, Easter Island is one of the newest mystery of an ancient civilization that disappeared into the ages. We are now looking beyond Easter Island's Statues towards the individuals, their lives and what might be the reason why they disappear.

Location

The island covers 64 square miles and is situated just more than 2,000 miles to the from Chile. Easter Island is also known as Rapa Nui.

The People

The people who lived there were immigrants. While they were there between 300-400 A.D there's no information about. There were kings in the area however, not much of their family ties or the way they regarded their elders is documented.

Cultural Contribution

We know that they lived through three distinct periods of culture. This is the time when are famous statues that anyone can be able to see were constructed in the islands. The majority of these statues were also burial places that housed the deceased. The majority of their history was characterized by various civil wars that began around 1680.

Beliefs and Religion

The tribe of Rapa Nui was a place where rituals were held for everything from birth until a child's first haircut and on. They would hold initiation ceremonies, and the moment when a member of the tribes got their first tattoos, it was a sacred occasion. They revered death as a part of their faith because they believed that their forefathers would return after their death to assist their tribe. They also believed that mana existed and magic.

Architecture and Technology

The majority of architecture was centered around their faith and reverence for dead people. They also constructed boats which looked like a reversed boat and buildings with rectangular floor plans. Researchers discovered about 250 houses on the higher areas of the island.

What was the cause?

In contrast to the other islands that have been mentioned, there is a consensus on the fact that they disappeared because of the overuse of the resources found on the island.

Chapter 6: Angkor

The town of Angkor Wat, located in Cambodia is awash in mystery and mysticism. While the technology was insufficient that could construct things like we do today however, they were able to build large and elaborate temples and towers. The first civilization to be established was the first half of the 12th century.

Location

It is located near Tonle Sap Lake and Northwest of Phnom Penh. It is situated in a dense forest, and it is hidden from sight. It is hidden in the forest and is considered to be a sacred area.

The People

They were adamant about their feeling of belonging. If a family required an apartment in the village, everyone from the village would gather and assist them in building their new home. They were a tightly knit community who helped each other out. We do know that they were a fervent religious military, agricultural, and religious people.

Cultural Contribution

Due to the mystery of their culture the culture of their people isn't very well-known.

Beliefs and religions

It is a subject of debate regarding the religious beliefs of the people of Angkor. Although the country is largely Buddhist There are Hindu symbols and motifs.

Architecture and Technology

At the time they were among the most sophisticated regarding architecture, due to their design by the sculptors at the time. They made creative use of stone in the temples homes, temples, and structures that were built around that of the temple's main.

What was the cause?

There are a variety of reasons that led to the popularity of Angkor.

-Trade

The time that a surge in shipping trade started this weakened the strategic importance of the city.

-Overpopulation

A lot of research pointed that the city was larger than the area that their town.

-Drought

A major change has taken place in the climate, which could lead to dry conditions in the region that could have contributed to the decline of the civilization.

My two points

Many believe it could have been one or more of these reasons It is better to describe a mix of the three that eventually resulted in this civilisation.

It's your turn

What are your thoughts about what was the cause?

What theories do you think are viable and what is the reason?

What theories do you think are weak? as weak and why?

The Incas Incas

Then we head towards South America for the next few civilizations. We'll start with the Incas who lived their lives and what transpired to them.

Location

The Incan Empire spanned across Northern Ecuador to central Chile. The region was home to more than 12 million people belonging to more than 100 ethnic groups during the height of its civilisation. It was referred to by the name of Tawantinsuyu as well as "Land of the Four Corners".

The people

The Incas were a thriving and diverse group of people as evident by the many ethnic groups.

They were renowned for their agricultural practices and the ability to sustain an unifying state. The monarchy was the basis in their government system. They used to practice mummification of their rulers as well as a lengthy oral history that is seen in their art as well. When they controlled different civilizations, they'd enforce their theocracy onto them. They were a society with plunderers, conquerors, and conquests.

Cultural Contributions

They had many contributions to the world and are renowned for their talent. They also held a firm faith in the concept of creation and a deep respect for their elders and leaders.

Beliefs and religions

People believed they had a god of the creator, Viracoha, who rose from the Pacific Ocean. He was the creator of all that they saw as he walked across Lake Titicaca including the sun and all the other people. They believed that they had been"the "Chosen Ones" having been the children of the Sun God with his name Inti. They believed that their leader was personification of the god. They heavily relied on divination to detect illness, assist in criminality solving, and also to predict the extent to which they would succeed in conflicts and wars.

Architecture and Technology

They were also known for their mastery of stonemasonry creating blocks with a fine finish no matter if they were your typical shape or polygonal. They worked them with such precision that they didn't require mortar when they were placed together. They built huge buildings, walls and fortifications were built with smooth surfaces and clean lines. They also employed mason's work to construct roads for transporting items. Their roads covered more than 4000 kilometers.

What has happened?

As you could imagine, due to their ferocious nature and the way they imposed their way of life on the people they conquered they weren't very well-liked. This was particularly true in their northern regions. They were faced with a myriad of rebellions. As the conquistadors began to invade upon their territories and encroach on their territory, they were afflicted with illnesses like small pox as well as other childhood illnesses, not having been exposed. The diseases inflicted on the people with around 90% of the population.

My two points

It was the perfect situation to bring down an entire civilization. You're not only having to deal with the constant resentments of people who didn't like how they were treated, but you had to contend with disease and invaders you've not had to deal with and put up a defense.

The Inca language is still spoken today although its population has diminished. There are numerous written records of their history and artwork, not forgetting to not forget their roads and buildings that are still in existence today.

The Minoans

It's impossible to discuss lost civilizations without traveling to Greece and describing the story of the Minoan Civilization. The Minoan Civilization grew at the start in the Bronze Age.

Location

In the past, civilizations were or vast expanses of land or compact areas and, with the exception of those of Rapa Nui, Minoans inhabited the area we now call The Isle of

Crete. It is one of the largest islands in the Mediterranean Sea, and being an island and a civilisation in this period it was a place that saw many advances.

The People

Evidence has been discovered that dates an era of Minoan inhabitants on Crete about 7700 BCE. The Minoan civilization was named by an archeologist who found their evidence. They named Minoan people after the king Minos. They were not organized in the same way as other civilizations. In the beginning they were decentralized, meaning there was no distinct distinction between classes or a governmental structure.

Cultural and contributions

In the early days, they did not have a set the culture. The palaces were in close proximity to the communities they served. They had tombs where they put their dead. Families and clans of all clans were laid to rest in the tombs with offerings to fill the space. Older remains that had become bone were relocated into bone chambers.

In the period between 1900 and 1700, things began to shift. The Minoans experienced an enormous shake-up that made the Minoans change their structure. In the year 2000 BCE was when the Minoans crown their first king, setting up the structure of a hierarchy. They believed they had a king they also had a bureaucracy established, that established the social order and class system for nobles, peasants, and perhaps slaves. In the year 1700 BCE the palaces were destroyed from the city by unknown forces.

Between 1700 and 1400 BCE In the period from 1700 to 1400 BCE, reconstruction took place and the buildings were more impressive than the previous ones. This was the time when the famed Knossos, Pahaistos, Malia Zakros Palaces that were constructed. Instead of palaces being constructed close to communities, towns were constructed near them. The dead were buried in pithoi, big and lengthy storage containers, and above-ground circular tombs. This was the first appearance of villas in the countryside. The villas were tiny palaces that contained storage spaces and workshop spaces, as well as worship areas.

Beliefs and Religion

It is not known much about their beliefs. The evidence suggests that the existence of minor male gods. The goddesses were the ones to be focused on in the religious system. They could identify an incarnation of the Mistress of Animals and an animal goddess as well as a household goddess, and many others that they were unable to be identified, however they speculated that these goddesses came to the Greek Pantheon as Hera, Artemis, and other goddesses.

Architecture and Technology

They made use of blocks of limestone and sandstone with crossbeams and rubble added to the mix. They were able to create stairs, doorjambs and benches. The walls were painted at times and even featured frescoes. The roofs of their homes were flat and constructed from wooden beams. They also invented stucco.

What has happened?

There are a variety of theories on what changed with what was once the Minoan culture.

Natural Disaster

There is evidence of the total destruction of Thera however experts disagree whether it was caused by the eruption or earthquakes, or tsunamis. Many believe it could be the combination of all three of these.

- Changing of the Guard

There is a theory that due to the possibility of disaster, the economic turmoil allowed the Mycenae to invade and conquer the Minoans.

My two points

I believe that all of these factors were a part of the mix to lead to the demise of the Minoans.

It's Your Turn

What did you think has happened?

What theories do you think that you can believe in and what is the reason?

What theories do you think are weak? as unsound and why?

The Anasazi

We're traveling to what's today in the United States to look at an entire group consisting of Native Americans who disappeared.

Location

You can tell from their map lived throughout New Mexico, some of Arizona and a lot more Colorado as well. Utah.

The People

These were among the very first group of people that were not nomadic. They created a community around the land and agriculture so that they could stay within a single location. They were taught to live and work in harmony. They were the pioneers among their fellow Native Americans of that time period.

Cultural and contributions

Their lives and their culture was centered around farming, crafting, and animal husbandry. They are famous in the pottery industry for its designs baskets woven and irrigation. They constructed roads to transport goods like their wood that was more than fifty miles distant. They were a matriarchal community and all wisdom and decisions for the development of civilizations were taken by women from the tribe.

Beliefs and Religion

They Anasazi had a polytheistic belief system. They worshipped patron gods who governed everything, from the rains to animals and crops. It was an earth-based religion. The worshippers would adore their gods with the hope of having a vibrant community. They believed that their rituals helped make them more attuned to the natural world. To practice this religion of nature they also had Shamans as holy individuals within their tribe.

Architecture and Technology

The Anasazi are famous for their design. Visit the cliff dwellings and observe how they were able create houses for themselves. They made use of wood taken from far away to build their houses. They also have a reputation for their irrigation systems as well as the roads they constructed. They also had the ability to design their own weapons for hunting or farm and defend themselves.

What has happened?

Although evidence suggests that they may have been a human race, there is a myriad of theories on the reason they vanished and fell.

Self Destructive

There is evidence that suggests they engaged in fighting among themselves. Archeologists and anthropologists suggest there was fighting, which could have led to civil wars as well as cannibalism.

-Drought

The evidence was found, thanks to the study of tree rings, of numerous droughts that occurred in succession with one lasting for 14 years. This makes it impossible to cultivate the food that they required to survive.

My two points

Tree rings record the physical record of the environmental. If they had to endure many droughts, it is a solid reason how they disappeared. This may have contributed to the fighting, as droughts also affect the livestock, which can cause problems for the Anasazi.

It's Your Turn

What are your thoughts about what was the cause?

What theories do you think are valid and what is the reason?

What theories do you consider as weak and why?

The Mycenaeans

We're returning to Greece to explore a different civilization that was lost without an explanation.

Location

As you will see, they lived throughout Greece. Their main cities included Mycenae, Tiryns, Argos, Sparta, and possibly Athens.

The People

The Mycenaean people prospered in the latter part of the Bronze Age. Their name derives of the city state that was most prominent within the region. They were a major part of craft, crafts, and even architecture.

Cultural and contributions

Thanks to the advances in technological advancements of the day and the advancements in technology, the Mycenaeans could create jewelry, frescoes, as well as the advancement of Greek language. Another aspect was the forming of city-states that organized towns into administrations.

Beliefs and Religion

There is not much information about their faith in general, however we know that they practiced the ritual of sacrifices to animals, most notably communal feasts, rituals of libation, and the offering of food. The excavations revealed double-axe carvings as well as consecration horns in the art and architecture. Altar frescoes have been discovered. They even made ritual swords and daggers.

Architecture and Technology

The ancient temples were centred around Megarons or a large rectangular central halls. This was the basis for what would later be Archaic or Classical Temples. The palace heart typically had smaller halls and private rooms for storage, administration and manufacturing.

They also learned black smithing and armor crafting.

What was the cause?

Another civilization is a mystery to why they vanished.

-Invasion

There is evidence from around 1500 BCE from the Mycenaeans expanding the dimensions of their wall. This could indicate increased conflict among the city-states , or perhaps an invasion from abroad. The authorities found burning buildings that were smashed by the people who came in after.

My Two Cents

I'm not sure of a solid theory, but it is possible that conflict could be the cause.

It's your turn

What are your thoughts about what was the cause?

What theories do you think that are plausible and what is the reason?

What theories do you consider as weak and why?

Chapter 7: How Do We Have A Clear Understanding Of Our History?

The history of the world is full of mystery, and it's quite possible that we don't know all of it. Consider the time scales involved. We are on a rock known as Earth that has been floating around space for more than the span of four billion. Human (or at the very least, human-like) existence on this planet is estimated to be around 2 million years.

A large portion of that time was, naturally, a place during the dark prehistoric age, before humans developed the capacity to record and write down accounts of their daily activities. Since there are no writing records of our earliest prehistoric past, the only thing option is to to look at the archaeological evidence in order to unravel the tale of these ancestors who were long gone.

For example, the Anasazi from the Four Corners region of the United States, for example lived in an enlightened society, but there was no written record of their lives it's the rocks around them which tell their tale. What a tale it is. The ancient people built whole cities out of walls of canyons, and over mesas. They even constructed roads to get through their huge complexes.

Even when ancient civilizations have written records that can be deciphered for example, like Mesoamerican Maya of Mesoamerica It can be extremely difficult to understand why they did what they did. The Maya were amazing astronomers and astronomy was a huge tool for ancient civilizations in the field of navigation and agriculture, but for the Maya it was more than that.

They constructed entire calendars around distant astronomical events that shouldn't have bothered them in the slightest. It's astonishing the things they were able accomplish, but one cannot not help but wonder what the reason was. Couldn't their energies have been better used to address the immediate issues of their time rather than anticipating celestial events to occur in the years after they'd died and gone?

The goals of the ancients could be difficult to understand. Another example is that the inhabitants of Easter Island were obsessed with the creation of massive stone structures that appeared to have no use. However, even as their community was under famine and other pressures from outside the islanders continued to make the building of these massive moai of stone a top prioritization. What's more interesting are those living in the Indus Valley in the modern day India/Pakistan who constructed highly developed urban areas (with flush toilets, not less!) but then saw them completely destroyed overnight by an unknown force.

This book aims to find the answers to these numerous questions to determine what we actually have to know about our past.

What happened to Neanderthals?

Before even discussing what could have happened to the Neanderthals it is essential to identify the Neanderthals? While many of us may are familiar with the image of an Neanderthal as a stereotyped caveman with a low-brow and a stooped back and grunting at a flame but the majority of us don't know more than the stereotype.

The fossil records suggest that the Neanderthals first appeared around 200 000 years ago. They were a primitive , vastly diverse species, their habitat was spread across Western Europe all the way to Asia.

First Neanderthal bones were discovered in Germany's Neander Valley, or as the Germans refer to the area, Neander Tal. It is possible to conclude that it was due to this fact that the people who had the bones would be forever referred to as Neanderthals.

The Neanderthals lived in quite difficult conditions. As a result of their survival in the Ice Age, they had to endure extreme cold as well as general environmental hardship. But somehow or some other way, Neanderthal society not only did well, but flourished in many areas of the coldest in Northern Europe and Asia.

While Neanderthals were not as primitive as they are generally portrayed as, they had the ability to design warm clothing from animals' skins (recent evidence suggests that they constructed feathered capes out of the carcasses of Vultures!) and also to know how to create fires in order to keep the chill at the bay. The artifacts that were recovered have now proved that Neanderthals knew how to create stone tools.

However, the Neanderthals were mostly hunter-gatherers. Unlike their Homo sapiens cousins, who at this time were already settling down and farming the land-- thus creating surplus crops to last during times of scarcity--Neanderthals spent pretty much all day, every day looking for their next meal. Homo sapiens, as they didn't have to be all day long searching for food, had the time to learn other abilities, like taming hunting dogs. This could give an advantage they finally met Neanderthals.

Indeed, some scientists like the historian Pat Shipman, have recently stuck to these dogs in an attempt to help explain the disappearance of the Neanderthals. Homo sapiens, together with domesticated animals, first appeared in the wild around 40 000 years ago, in the middle that the decline began for Neanderthals. This has been the basis for Shipman to speculate that we small-minded Homo sapiens may have cut our dogs into Neanderthals who were hapless and effectively killed the whole lot.

However, before we blame Fido it is important to not forget that other scientists have noted that the advent of Homo sapiens could have forced Neanderthals from their natural habitat and food sources. In this case, the Neanderthals were simply forced to their caves by more adapted humans and then slowly perished from lack of nutrition.

Some, however argue that modern humans were not accountable, either intentionally or unintentionally for the disappearance of Neanderthals. They believe that the Neanderthals weren't driven to extinction , but rather to interbreed. The theory is that, when Homo sapiens came into contact with Neanderthals and the two species started to crossbreed in such a way that the Neanderthals were entirely absorbed into Homo sapiens lineage. Genetic studies have proved that the majority of Europeans and Asians contain anywhere from 2 to 5 percent Neanderthal DNA. This suggests the fact that Homo humans and Neanderthals were able to date one another (over an enjoyable woolly mammoth dinner, perhaps?) at some point in the past, possibly even before the beginning of time.

It is possible that many factors played a role in the decline of the Neanderthals. Perhaps their inability to compete against more advanced humans, as well as interbreeding and frequent interbreeding, as well as another factor, climate change, weighed the Neanderthals in. Yes, there is climate change. Although it's an issue of current concern it's been happening since Earth was a planet with an atmosphere and the idea that this could impact human environments is not an entirely new idea. Consider the stark differences between Earth in the past Ice Age and now, and you'll see that the climate of our planet has seen a few changes in the environment before.

Geologists suggest that one significant change in the world might have influenced the Neanderthal approximately 40 000 years ago. Particularly, it has been reported that a huge eruption of volcanic ash in Italy called"the "Campanian Ignimbrite eruption" could have caused a rapid cooling as high as 4 degrees due to the massive quantity of ash and soot that was released across Europe. It was then followed by more devastating acid rain. Could this environmental catastrophe be the catalyst for the Neanderthal dying off?

The theory that will be most applicable to the 2021 pandemic-ravaged world is the possibility that Homo sapiens, who recently quit their home on the African continent, may have brought along a fatal virus that people of Neanderthal descent from Europe were not immune to in their natural state. If that's the case, it won't be the only instance of a new illness that has decimated the culture that had never been was exposed. In the Americas for instance it was there were more Native Americans perished from European diseases than were killed by the hand of colonizers and conquistadors.

However, a new research conducted by a group of Canadian researchers from the Montreal's McGill University claims that the tiny fraction that is Neanderthal DNA that the majority of us have actually produce proteins that can aid in fighting disease. Particularly the case of an Neanderthal protein known as OAS1 increases immunity. They also declare that the higher the proportion of Neanderthal DNA a person has, the better their chance of beating the latest human scourge, COVID-19. COVID patients who have greater OAS1 levels OAS1 are reportedly less likely to require hospitalization in the event of contracting with coronavirus.

There's a lot we don't know about Neanderthals. However, as bizarre of an era as their time on earth might be they certainly left a legacy that will last forever. Since the majority of us carry our DNA's sequences just a tiny portion of them will remain until the time that humanity is.

The Lost Civilization of Atlantis

The mysterious civilisation of Atlantis. Perhaps no other known culture is so mysterious as this mysterious locale. Atlantis is so elusive, in fact, nobody is able to figure out if it actually existed. The first reference to the fabled civilization comes through Plato, the Greek philosopher Plato. Within one of his lengthy philosophical dialogues written in the year the year 360 BC, Plato spoke of the great island nation known as Atlantis which existed 10,000 years before.

According to Plato the society of that time was the best the world ever experienced.

The inhabitants were so wealthy that they were able to afford everything they ever desired. But somewhere along the lines, things got out of hand and the "gods got angry" with them. Atlantis was submerged and fell into the sea. Plato further stated that the people who lived there were gods in their own right, meaning they were half human and divine. Plato went on to say his belief that god Poseidon himself created Atlantis by taking a normal human woman as his bride and thus establishing the Atlanteans.

However, the majority of experts believe that it was just an allegory Plato employed to warn his followers about the risks of living a life of excess similar to what the Atlanteans did. The idea about being the Greek god Poseidon being the father of Atlanteans seems to be something more or less Greek myth, infused with Plato's original and imaginative storytelling. But what if the Founder was not Poseidon or a different type of superior being that Plato was not able to explain?

As fantastical as the entire Poseidon part is, a lot of the fundamental details seem more like a real physical description than just an imaginative story. Plato says that the Atlantis's landmass Atlantis was approximately as big as Libya in the Mediterranean and Asia Minor (modern-day Turkey) together, which is roughly similar to Australia. The landmass was surrounded by purposefully constructed rings of water and land that served as barriers against invaders. These land-based rings featured numerous checkpoints, which included gates and watchtowers. Only allowed vessels could enter. It's only been recent that humans are beginning to construct artificial islands. Was this an example of land engineering from the past?

In any case the specifics that Plato offered to describe Atlantis appear a little too complex for something that was simply an allegory. They appear to be an attempt to provide an accurate description of an actual place. What is the reason Plato spend all the trouble of saying that Atlantis was an island Atlantis was located west of Pillars of Hercules (the Strait of Gibraltar) even if there was never a landmass there? If he was inventing an imaginary story, wouldn't he selected a place close to home, like the Mediterranean maybe, instead of all the way across the Atlantic Ocean?

In addition, if we find out that there's actually some truth in the Atlantis legend, it won't it be the first instance an ancient city believed to be a myth was proved to be true. For centuries, the world's scholars believed that Troy was a mythical city. Troy was simply an epoch for Greek mythology concerning the Trojan war, until archaeologists unearthed the remains of this once great city and were forced admit that the city existed in reality.

What do you think of Atlantis? Does it seem possible that there was really a lost civilization that was buried under the waves? If there were a landmass located in between the Atlantic this would help solve many of the questions that are being asked about the recent evidence that the early peoples of America could have had contacts with the ancient civilizations in Africa or Europe.

Historical scholars have for years tried to deny the existence of such a possibility, however archaeological evidence found in

North as well as South America seem to indicate that there was some kind of transatlantic connection between the continents before Christopher Columbus sailed the ocean blue. Mummies from Egypt for instance, have been discovered to contain tiny amounts of both cacao and tobacco, two plants that originated within the Americas and were believed to be undiscovered by the people of the rest around the globe prior to Columbus's expedition around 1492 AD. How can the Old World mummy from 5,000 years ago be able to have these on its mummified body?

It's important to note that the first source from the source from which Plato discovered the facts regarding Atlantis was an Greek official and diplomat called Solon who was able to get the story directly from Egyptians. Of obviously, if the tale was derived from the Egyptians then they would not have referred to that Greek god Poseidon as the god of Atlantis. As we've previously mentioned that the Poseidon idea is by far the weakest element of the story of Plato. It's likely that he added it to make it a more familiar reference by using

"Poseidon" to create within the mind of the readers the powerful god of the oceans.

In any case the fact that the ancient Egyptians were found to have products that came from the other side of the Atlantic strongly suggests some kind of trade between the old earth and New World. The next question, however is how this movement between continents occurred. Sailboats? It was a difficult journey to Columbus in 1492. It would have been nearly impossible to the Egyptians. What would they do if they didn't need to go as far? What if there were an island between Africa and the Americas, a continent known as Atlantis?

Atlantis could have served as an effective intermediary trading goods between continents, or as a point of entry to travelers between the continents. With the vastness of Atlantis situated between two continents, the Americas as well as the other continents in the Old World, rather than long journeys across uncharted oceans, it would be a simple hop, skip and a leap from one continent to the next. It's interesting to consider that in Plato's first story, he refers to the idea of an "enormous continent" accessible from the opposite part of Atlantis. Okay, it could have an unintentional idea on the part of Plato, but maybe it was not.

If Atlantis was real What was its fate? In the words of Plato the entire civilization was destroyed within "a one day and night of tragedy." This has always pleased Atlantis Skeptics, who laugh at the idea that a whole continent could be submerged in one day. However, Plato further reveals about the fact that Atlanteans were a race of people who harnessed incredible powers. They were believed to have used crystal-based reactors which could generate enormous quantities of energy. Could it be this amazing power that caused the destruction of Atlantis? Could it have created an earthquake that shattered the seafloor and then dragged Atlanteans into it? Atlanteans in?

It may sound a bit far-fetched However, a "Type 1" civilization might actually be able to accomplish this. The Kardashev scale was created by Russian scientist Nikolai Kardashev describes the term "Type 1" as one that harnesses energy in such a way as to regulate the entire globe's "natural force." The type 1 civilization would therefore be able to regulate the weather patterns, alter geophysical features, and even trigger earthquakes.

In Plato's narrative in Plato's story, the Atlanteans were given this kind of knowledge and advanced understanding from Poseidon (a god also famous for causing earthquakes and storms). Instead of using their power to benefit others, they been able to dominate the smaller nations around them. In reality they were said to have conquered the majority areas of North Africa and Western Europe. They were in the midst of dominating the entire world as an alliance between the last independent states gathered to fight the Atlantean giant. Athens, the Greek city-state of Athens was part of this alliance and, when all the other states were defeated by the Atlanteans, it was Athens Athenians who stood up for themselves in the face of Atlanteans.

Despite any odds, the Athenians won. And immediately after massive earthquakes, flooding and all kinds of other events resulted in Atlantis to sink under the waves. The cataclysmic catastrophe was so catastrophic that it made the entire area of the Atlantic Ocean "unnavigable and unexplorable."

It is important to consider this as well, since the famous psychic Edgar Cayce would later claim that the source of Atlantis's power lay by manipulating crystals that were powerful that were the energy source that ultimately ended up making havoc across the Atlantic Ocean.

Through his dreams of old Atlantis, Cayce saw a huge crystal-based power station that was housed in a dome-shaped structure that the Atlanteans employed to generate power. The demise of Atlantis was reportedly due to a failure of the reactor (or maybe it was destroyed by a clever Athenian?). The well-guarded crystal power source unleashed an incredibly powerful blast of energy that caused the entire continent to sink beneath the ocean. According to Cayce that some Atlantean refugees were able to escape to Egypt where they reconstructed the story in the Egyptian archives--the same source from where Solon claimed to have heard the tale, but the majority were killed during the cataclysm.

Cayce believed that energy bursts occasionally appear from the wreckage of Atlantis and that these powerful explosions could cause planes and ships to vanish. The mysterious disappearances are believed to occur in a cryptic tiny part of the Atlantic that has come to be referred to as The Bermuda Triangle. Many have also suggest that the western end of Atlantis might have been located close to the current Bermuda Triangle.

Cayce herself made the shocking prediction that a portion of Atlantis would be discovered many years later after his demise. many believe that the prophecy is already coming to realization. Cayce passed away in the year 1945 and the known as "Bimini Road" was discovered in the year 1968. Bimini Road Bimini Road is an unusual and a road-like, artificial structure located off on the shores of Bimini Island in the Bahamas. At the time of date, Bimini Road is an anomaly that is not fully explained. It could constitute an element of the architecture of an unidentified civilization. But what is that unknown civilization? Could it be a tiny remnant of the mythical Atlantis? The mystery continues to be solved.

Nuclear Fallout in the Indus Valley

The Indus Valley Civilization grew in the vicinity of Indus Valley (now northwestern India and southeastern Pakistan) in the year 7000 BC. This is the region that is now barren. an ancient civilization flourished with cities that were fully developed.

Indus Valley Civilization Indus Valley Civilization can also be known as Harappan Civilization. Harappan Civilization due to its connection to Harappa as a city. Harappa. The chronology of this active society is often divided into the following epochs

* Pre-Harappan (7000 BC--5500 BC)
* The early Harappan (5500 BC - 2800 BC)
*Mature Harappan (2800 BC - 1900 BC)
* The late Harappan (1900 BC - 1500 BC)
* Post-Harappan (1500 BC--600 BC)

The Harappan/Indus Valley Civilization was least the same level of development as Mesopotamia and pre-historic Egypt but in many instances may have even surpassed their the development. As remarkable as it was, its existence was largely forgotten by history for a considerable period in the dust of the past until it was discovered around 100 years in the past. The knowledge that has been uncovered in the intervening time is simply amazing.

The technology of this society was quite advanced for its age. Cities actually had functional wastewater facilities, and private houses even were equipped with an early flush toilets, which allowed the inhabitants to dump their garbage into an aqueduct, which was later discharged out of the city. The Indus Valley home was also with "wind catchers" that were put on the roof to keep the air moving into the building. Archaeologists were pleasantly surprised to discover this early model of "air conditioning" on such a dated location, but it's true that the Indus Valley is packed with surprising discoveries.

In fact the more they've uncovered concerning the valley of the Indus the more historians are forced to change what they believed they knew about the past. The two major archaeological sites are Harappa and a second major city named Mohenjo-daro. "Known for" because, despite the fact that the city was once home to the population of 50,000 people but no one knows the name it had. The name Mohenjo-daro was lent to this city in the hands of the people who first discovered it. Translated roughly to mean "Mound of the dead." It's not exactly the most glamorous name for a grand urban civilization of old, but it stuck.

Alongside Harappa and Mohenjodaro, the Indus Valley Civilization was once boasting an estimated population of millions. However, something changed. In the year 1900 BC the once-great and bustling society was beginning to decline. There is speculation that neighboring tribes from the north could have invaded and wiped it with force. This is certainly possible and, more importantly even as large that The Indus Valley Civilization it never any standing army as well as even the most basic of defenses. It was much more of an open field for anyone who could gather sufficient numbers and would have been willing to take trips into in the Indus Valley to fight.

It is important to note another aspect regarding the settlements in the Indus Valley: they aren't constructed and positioned in the same manner as other sites of ancient civilizations. Most of the time, these the ancient settlements are constructed in a piecemeal manner. A temple is constructed with a few homes along with a bathhouse, and several more houses -- it's an ongoing process that spans several years. The interesting thing about settlements that are located in the Indus Valley is that they appear to have been built at approximately the same at the same time. It seems as if a person with enormous resources and strength was able to simply arrive on the scene and began to build entire cities based on a meticulously planned blueprint, which is a very unusual way of construction at this period. The buildings were constructed with a common focus on their intended use and, for some reason, the plans for construction didn't include the city wall or any defense structures of any kind.

Another explanation for the reason why that the Indus Valley Civilization was in decline is the same one that was used by numerous other dying civilizations: the danger from climate changes. There is a belief that this region started to experience severe droughts in the past and that the primary water source was that is the Sarasvati River, all but disappeared. This would have not only resulted in the people being without water for drinking, but could also have caused all their meticulously irrigated crops to get dry and die away.

A single of the more absurd explanations for the loss of Indus Valley Civilization it is nothing more than atomic war. Yes I know that it sounds absurd. Nuclear weapons in the old world? Why would anyone bother to make such an assertion? As absurd as it sounds it is, there are some bizarre anomalies found on the website that seem to confirm it.

In the beginning, unexplained amounts of radiation was observed at the location. It was enough to set the conspiracy wheels turning. And then there's the "mound of the deceased." The name isn't just a flimsy one. Another interesting aspect of this archeological site is that you could actually see mounds and mounds containing people who appear to have been killed in one go. Combine this with the radiation, and the imaginations started to get wild. Then people began to envision the massive nuclear explosion that killed every one of the Indus Valley inhabitants simultaneously: "Oh, those poor Harappans of the past didn't know the exact cause of their deaths after being blasted into the point of extinction. They were burned to death while sitting at their table to eat tea or taking an enjoyable bath in the bathhouse. They were instantly killed, in the exact spot they were by an old A-bomb."

A few, it should be noted have suggested that the burial mounds of the deceased were simply burial mounds. However, the strange placement of the bones do not seem to be in line with how the majority of ancient peoples laid their bodies to rest. The ancients, much as we do today were meticulous in the proper burials. The typical burial was to lay the body of the deceased on their backs, and then lay their hands on their chests. The bodies that were discovered in these graves, however were discovered in various odd positions. Some of them were lying on their stomachs or on their sides and some lying on their backs like they were blown backwards. Some looked as if they had been thrown out of their chairs, and then died in the sitting posture (tea anyone?).

To make things more fascinating is an old Sanskrit work dubbed the Mahabharata which describes cities as the tragic Mohenjo-daro getting destroyed by a variety of mystical weapons that sound remarkably like nuclear bombs. One of the passages from the Mahabharata is about a war that was a disaster in northern India. The war is similar to a full-on nuclear war:

A single projectile that is charged with the full potential of our universe. A glowing column of flame and smoke as brilliant as the sun's thousand stars sat in all its glory. It was a weapon that was not known, an iron thunderbolt. It was a massive messenger to death... that diminished to the ashes... all the race Vrishnis as well as the Andhakas... They bodies were so burned to disappear... Hair and nails fell off... The pottery broke with no apparent reason... and the birds were turned into white... In some time, all food items were affected... To get away from the blaze, the soldiers threw themselves into streams to wash themselves as well as their equipment.

This is remarkably similar to the results of a nuclear explosion, where those who do not instantly disintegrate (as evidently the entire population of Vrishnis as well as the Andhakas was) are exposed to radioactive fallout that causes their nails and hair falling out. Foods are also affected by the leftover radiation from an atomic explosion. Even the opening sentence regarding the "projectile that is charged with the full force of the universe" as big as it sounds is true to it, because the splitting of an atom does indeed harness the fundamental forces in the universe in itself.

Then there's the tale of soldiers jumping into waters to cleanse their equipment and themselves of the nuclear fallout. It was exactly the same thing in Japan at the close of World War Two, when the atomic bombs fell upon Hiroshima in Nagasaki and Hiroshima. Nagasaki. Also survivors were found jumping into the water in desperate attempts to wash off the radiation which was burning their skin.

I'm not affirming that a nuclear explosion destroyed this Indus Valley Civilization however considering the anecdotal anomalies the Harappans' final death certainly seems odd. Perhaps, someday, we'll discover a crucial clue, and then we'll be able to tell what happened, but until then, we'll have to speculate.

Petrified in Petra

The Nabataean Civilization

The Nabataean civilization is rooted in the agitated Bedouin community from Arabs who eventually found their way to the present-day site of Jordan which is where they established Petra, the capital city. Petra which later became their capital city. The city is distinctive because it was built from the side of an mountain. It was certainly a unique location to build an urban area, however the Nabataeans expert engineers could pull off and the rock wall surrounding it was an effective defense against visitors who were not invited.

Petra reached its peak at the beginning of one hundred years ago in the first century

AD. Under their king, Aretas IV the Nabateans enjoyed prosperity, and expressed their appreciation by constructing an elaborate mausoleum that later came to be known as al-Khazneh (the Treasury) because it was home to all kinds of treasure within its stone walls. The most remarkable thing about Petra however, was how the Nabateans created dams, conduits, and cisterns to ensure they could make use of rainwater in times of drought. This was, naturally extremely useful in the desert conditions of the region.

The kingdom began to decline, but the Romans took control in the year 106 AD. The Nabateans were friendly to the Romans for a long time and even the famous Emperor Herod from Judea (just consider the famous Christmas Nativity story) is the child of the Nabataean princess. However, eventually, the friendship didn't suffice for the Romans and in 106 AD, they added the Nabataean Kingdom directly to the Roman Empire. The Romans added their own stamps on Petra by constructing Roman-style gates as well as additional structures within the sprawling.

Roman rule was interrupted by a devastating earthquake during the 4th century which destroyed many of these structures. However, it was the Romans' Byzantine Empire successors ultimately retook the city and reigned for several hundred years more before announcing their departure. From that point on it was the Nabataean civilization of Petra was declining until the city that legends tell of into the rock's face disappeared completely. In the end, only a handful of nomad shepherds who were able to make use of its ruin as a temporary shelter when passing through the region were aware the existence of Petra.

It was discovered only after Johann Ludwig Burkhardt, a Swiss explorationist, stumbled upon the site in 1812. Burkhardt was a 27-year-old adventurous type of person, and when he learned that an German researcher had been victimized by bad luck when trying to locate the city that was mysterious He decided to attempt to find the city by himself. He was bold, brave or even just plain crazy, he was determined to locate Petra. He ensured that he did the research first in the process of opening his own business at Cairo, Egypt, he was able to study the Arab culture and language until he was sure that he would fit into the culture without being able to be viewed (or identified) by the outsiders. He even went as that he took on the Arabic name, naming him sheikh Ibrahim Ibn Abdallah. While seamlessly blending with the people of the area, Burkhardt made his way through Jordan until he came to the largely deserted site of Petra.

The city that was once a ghost town is now a major tourist destination as well as a UNESCO World Heritage Site. Numerous other discovery have taken place over the years which includes the recovery of Byzantine scrolls in the late 1990s that provided a great insight into what the area was like at the time that was the Byzantine Empire. A brand-new monument was also discovered recently, hidden beneath levels of soil and rubble. It is believed to be the remains of a temple, whereas others believe it was an important political gathering where the Nabateans debated current issues. It appears that the marvels of Petra have just begun to be revealed.

The Unknown Minoans
The Minoan civilization was a part of Crete. Crete between 3000 to 1450 BC. Minoans are often mentioned as the first modern civilization in Europe. Similar to they had Mideastern as well as Near Eastern counterparts, they created impressive structures. Minoans are renowned for their magnificent palaces of four stories that were adorned with stunning, intricate frescoes.

It is mostly from these frescoes that we can get an impression of the Minoan living was. The frescoes portray people and women doing their day-to-day activities in a vivid manner. Bulls are prominently represented throughout the entire scene, and it is believed that bulls were a sacred animal to Minoans, who revered its strength and fertility. There are numerous frescoes that depict the Minoan ritual wherein minoans actually "grab the bull's horns"--after which they turn over on its back. It was surely an incredible sight to watch these bull riders in action, however it wasn't just for entertainment, it was also an essential aspect of their religion.

Another thing archaeologists have observed regarding Minoan civilization is the fact that it may be a matriarchal. Women played an important role in the religious system and the government during Minoan society. Minoan civilization. It is an extremely rare characteristic, since the majority of societies at that time were strict patriarchal. However, this was not the case on Crete. Ministers from the Minoan religion be largely female and the entire religion has embraced feminine forms with a manner that is shocking in comparison to its contemporary counterparts. In particular, while other religions generally viewed menstrual females as "unclean" however, the Minoans were openly celebrating the feminine aspect of life.

One theory about what actually occurred with Minoan civilization is that Minoan culture is that people became bored of living in a matriarchal society and decided to revolt against it. Did there actually exist a sort of real battle of the sexes that was going on between the Minoan people of the past? Perhaps. But it's just an idea that has not been proven to be true. is no proof to support it.

However the Minoans were a thriving and vibrant civilisation for many years. Minoan settlements were extremely advanced for their and time. The Minoans even used an early version of indoor plumbing, which is uncommon in the early world. The Minoans also employed tools, created art and had their own style of writing. They connected to the rest of the world through an extensive trade network that spanned the Mediterranean and to the Near East. They were adept in the field of trade and mercantilism from the time of their civilisation's beginning at around 3000 BC and it is believed that they were the first merchants that eventually developed into the royalty that resided in the palaces.

The period known as the "Middle Minoan" period, which started in the year 1800 BC and saw significant changes. It appears that a major catastrophe may be taking place whether it was an invading force from external sources or an eruption of volcanic ash that destroyed many palaces. The Minoans were able bounce back quickly however, and new palaces were built. It is believed that the Minoan civilization of that time was a major influence on the nearby Greece and began to imitate Minoan style of living. It was a good time on Crete even after another volcano erupted around 1600 BC that killed a lot of people and destroying other infrastructure, the powerful Minoans came back to rebuild their towns larger and better than they had ever been. A hundred years of development were followed.

Then, all of a sudden Minoans disappeared from the history of. The Minoans' death could have been through an attack from mainland Greece or in the form of a massive volcanic eruption. However, as of today the exact cause of what was the fate of the Minoans remains an open question.

What was the significance of Nabta Playa Civilization?

It is situated within The Nubian Desert of the forgotten culture that is Nabta Playa gets its name due to the fact that it is situated on several "playas" or, in other words dry lakes.

There wasn't always a lot of rain in this area, however. The first settlements of the Nabta Playa civilization have been dating back to 7500 BC and research suggests that the region had plenty of rain at that time. The area that is now a desert could be more like the Savanna. Also, there was a massive drainage basin, located around 500 miles to the south from Cairo, Egypt, which was able to hold water and functioned as a sort of irrigation system during dry seasons.

All this water was likely to have been home to a variety of animals, and it appears that this is what drove the initial settlements in the area. The first people to settle there were probably pastoralists who looked after cattle that roamed the grasslands in the area. There is also evidence to suggest that their faith was centered around cattle too. They definitely burned cattle as sacrifices during their rituals of worship; in fact, they built an entire underground "Valley of Sacrifices" in order to house the remains of sacrifices.

The cattle cult is connected to the Egyptian Hathor worship, which is centered around the goddess Hathor who is sometimes depicted in Egyptian artworks in the form of an animal. If they are related, it means that the more ancient Nabta Playa civilization was the source of this particular god along with other aspects of what evolved into the much-loved ancient Egyptian civilization.

Archaeological excavations have also confirmed that the people from Nabta Playa made extensive use of wild grain sorghum. Sorghum was and remains the mainstay of the African continent. The nature of the Nabta Playa sites contain some of the oldest evidence of it adds a fascinating aspect to their tale. Sorghum is a tough plant that is able to thrive in semi-arid climates, making it a perfect plant for Nabta Playa civilization. However, in the event that there would be a shortage in the future the inhabitants from Nabta Playa constructed copious cellars to store their surplus grain. This surplus was a way to maintain their community's vitality and let them pursue other interests.

One of the other hobbies was a love of stargazing. The inhabitants who lived in Nabta Playa had a keen fascination with Astronomy. The large stones were set in alignment with different star systems as well as other celestial objects. Much like Stonehenge, they identified the seasons and also the solstice of winter and summer. However, they didn't stop there. did.

There is evidence that suggests that the inhabitants in Nabta Playa used the stones to assist them in their task of traversing the desert. Satellite imagery has shown there were two lines of stone situated in the center of a circle were used to mark north/south and east/west directions. It is suggested that this type of navigation was vital for Nabta Playa people. Nabta Playa people because it helped them locate other playsas (lake beds) that were filled up during the rainy season. In the event that one of their lakes was dry the Nabta Playa people simply relied on their navigational aids based on stars to guide their boats to the next source of water.

Chapter 8: Enigmatic Easter Island

The strange piece of land located in the South Pacific that came to be known as Easter Island was first found by European explorators in 1722. The island was empty at the time but stones sentinels (moai) present everywhere indicated that it was once. The moai were huge structures comprised of a torso as well as heads that were massive, having similar facial characteristics. Because there were so many of them, and because they were so meticulously designed, it was evident that they were essential in the lives of the inhabitants. Also, since each statue were a few tons in weight and were quite heavy, they weren't easily to build and moved. They would've been a challenge even with the latest equipment and without it, huge labor and time would have been required.

Why did they did it? If we look deeper into the background and the story of this ancient civilization might find some clues.

The island was dubbed Easter Island due to the fact that it happened on Easter Sunday in 1722 when an Dutchman known as Jacob Roggeveen first landed on the island. While the islanders who lived there were scarce and infrequent the team of Roggeveen quickly came in contact with them and set out to gain as much knowledge about the area in the best way they could. They discovered that the natives used to call the island of the island was Te Pito Te Henua, which translates to "The Navel of the World." It seemed to Roggeveen to be quite a lofty title for an island that was almost uninhabited and the present inhabitants were unable to explain why they chose to call the island this. They couldn't even determine the purpose behind the huge moai.

However, they did have an intriguing story of the way their ancestors originally originated from an unknown island that was submerged beneath the ocean. We're not talking about Atlantis this time, we're talking about a lesser-known location that the Easter Islanders called Hiva. According to this piece of legend, the inhabitants of Hiva were warned of the catastrophe. After a priest gave the word to them that they were required to go, the Hivaites took their belongings and embarked on their journey towards Easter Island.

There is no way to verify this bizarre tale archaeologists have established the date of the first settlements on Easter Island to circa 400 AD. The island is quite remote situated about 2,237 miles to the to the west of it's South American mainland and some 1,100 miles from the closest other Island, Pitcairn. The most plausible guess that researchers have come up with regarding the islanders' history is that they are to Polynesia which is why they ended up on Easter Island after hundreds of years of island-hopping throughout oceans across the Pacific Ocean.

After a little research It was later discovered that the huge moai were constructed out of stones taken from a rock quarry within the center of an active volcano. It is believed that the creation of the statues was a process that lasted for many centuries and likely lasted up to at least the 17th century AD. The islanders somehow relocated these huge rocks across the island, putting them on the shoreline with their backs towards the ocean, looking at the interior like they were keeping watch. These stone sentinels don't appear to be protecting themselves from external threats, but rather, they're stone-faced guardians of Easter Island's residents.

What was their method of moving their bodies? There was an oral tradition of the Easter Islanders which stated that the statues "walked" over the islands. The majority of people believed that this was just a fantasy story, but in the year 2011, it offered two American researchers --Terry Hunt and Lipo--an idea. They came up with a method two groups of people who were able to pull ropes that were tied around the head of the statue. This, in actual gave the appearance it was as if the sculpture was walking while it moved slowly forward by twisting and rocking movements. This was not just a way to explain the story but also proved that it was been possible for the islanders to relocated the statues their on their own. However, moving a thousand statues using such a laborious procedure would certainly take a long time!

The islanders seemed to be obsessed with the building of these giant stone statues.

Evidence from archaeology suggests evidence that Easter Island once had a vast forest, however destruction of the forest caused problems regarding the soil. This made it hard to cultivate enough crops for the island's inhabitants. However, even with the growing issues, the creation of stone statues appears to be the main priority for the island.

As the island's resources became more and more scarce but its population began to experience a dramatic decline. There were just 3000 people living in Easter Island at the time of the first landing by Jacob Roggeveen in 1722. The situation went from bad to worse. A British expedition that was sent in 1774 discovered that the island's population had decreased to only a handful of hundred.

Combining the stories of oral traditions and archaeological excavations, it is apparent to be that Easter Islanders had erupted into an unrest between two factions known as The Short-Ears and Long Ears. Did this war bring down the islanders? Perhaps their society gradually deteriorate due to the loss of forests? It is unclear why this particular island exists. being solved.

The Anasazi
The First Ancient Aliens?

The Anasazi are a mysterious group. The name itself comes from an Navajo word, which literally means "ancient aliens." Although we're not making any claims about whether or not those Anasazi people were aliens but their culture is so obscure to us that it could be. Because they did not leave a written record, our only knowledge of the mysterious civilization comes from the archeological evidence rather than the archaeological record.

The Anasazi were located in their home in the Four Corners region of the southwest United States, near the junction of modern-day Colorado, Utah, Arizona as well as New Mexico. The most prominent geological feature of the region includes the Colorado Plateau, which comprises massive rock formations that are on top of vast mesas, flat mesas, and deep canyons. With this backdrop of ruggedness The Anasazi constructed impressive stone homes over the mesas and cut out of the walls of rock.

This may have been intended to be for defense purposes. The Anasazi themselves used ladders and ropes to get to their dwellings. When they were secure and safe in their stone homes they could easily remove the ladders and ropes and continue their daily lives with no fear of any intruders who might attack them.

There was a Anasazi civilization was built around these buildings, lasting for approximately 1000 years, before the settlements were dissolved about 1300 AD. The structures were pretty uniform in appearance and also contained similar baskets and tools, made in a fashion that is distinctive to the region.

The Anasazi were also fantastic road builders. Many of their structures were connected by roads. When we refer to "roads" we are referring to roads. They weren't just plain trails and causeways, but instead causeways that were around 30 feet wide, which is the exact width of current two-lane roadways. Anthropologists didn't expect to find such a thing which is why the majority of these roads weren't recognized as their significance until the introduction of satellite imagery.

It's unclear the purpose of these roads to serve, aside from the heavy foot traffic, however the Anasazi roads were massive in size. It stretched for about 180 miles across every direction, and had roads running from the canyon's bottoms upwards, through ramps and up to mesas and eventually going up to the tops of mountains. There has been a joke that the prehistoric Anasazi might be the owners of their very own vehicles to drive around roads, however since no evidence of vehicles was ever found the most likely reason for the existence of roads is to make it easier to transport stone construction materials from quarries.

According to the archeological record the civilization was in its peak between 800 to 1300 AD. This time period witnessed a dramatic increase in the complexity of construction that was characterized by highly skilled and skilled brickwork. The most precious stones were transported from faraway to construct huge complexes that in one instances had rooms big enough to accommodate many hundreds. What were these huge amphitheaters for? Some have suggested they were used for storage of food items, while others argue that they were places of worship for the gods. However, no one knows for sure.

One of the most bizarre aspects in Anasazi architectural design are Petroglyphs (rock drawings) which can be seen within the walls Anasazi structures. There are geometric designs , and even what appears to be spiral images that depict the solar system and also bizarre and awe-inspiring figures that aren't quite human. Anyone who is who is familiar of those who are familiar with the Ancient Aliens/Astronauts genre would guess the strange images have been the source of a myriad of conspiracy theories regarding the Anasazi. One of the characters is, for instance, that looks very much like someone wearing space suits. The sketch shows a massive figure sporting what appears to be an outer space helmet, along with the other gear of a person who is ready to explode into space.

But regardless of whether the Anasazi were in contact with the ancient spacecrafts, or no, they were surely talented as astronomers. They had a refined understanding of celestial objects and they meticulously tracked the moon, stars and sun as well as other planets. However, the fact that they were aware of the movement of celestial objects does not mean they were searching for aliens. Most likely, they used the science of astronomy to keep on top of the seasons for purposes of agriculture.

Interesting as their road systems and petroglyphs are most intriguing thing about the Anasazi is the fact that, at a time at a time when the civilization seemed to be at its peak their inhabitants vanished completely without clear explanation. The final years of Anasazi ought to have been great ones, according to archaeologists. Actually, they seemed to have lived life in the luxurious lifestyle. The treasures of high-valued objects like seashells and turquoise as well as exotic bird species have been discovered. All things that were useful trade goods in the time of this period. Additionally, even though it is true that the Four Corners region has semi-desert terrain, it is also home to a lot of ponderosa pine and juniper trees that date back up to Anasazi period. Additionally, the tree rings indicate that there was a lot of rain during this time period, which suggests that the Anasazi likely had abundant harvests and a plentiful food supply.

However, their civilization vanished but they are their descendants, the present-day Pueblo people--who reside in the area today. The Pueblo appear to come from Anasazi in the year 1400 AD at the time they began pushing further into territory that was previously occupied of the Four Corners region. We know these two cultures are interconnected because some of the practices of the Anasazi were passed down to the Pueblo. For instance the Anasazi constructed underground dugouts that were accessible via a ladder, to hold ceremonies There were Pueblo people who continue to continue to practice this tradition.

The mystery of what transpired to the Anasazi their people is not over. It gets even more intriguing when you consider that numerous ancient indigenous American civilizations mysteriously disappeared in a similar manner. To give only the most well-known example of this, the Maya certainly flourished when they left their magnificent temples in perfect condition and vanished completely from the Earth.

These things are so difficult to explain that they've been the source of wild theories about everything from alien abductions and time-travel (yes indeed, it has been proposed). However, as frustrating as it might be for us what we can say at this point is that we don't know.

The Olmecs

The Amazing Wonderfulness of Men of Rubber

At the height of their culture the Olmecs from the beginning had the highest power people in Mesoamerica. They were the precursors to more advanced civilizations like those of the Aztec as well as the Maya and their name is taken from their Aztec spoken language Nahuatl. The Aztecs refer to the Olmecs' territory Olmecs as Olman which translates to "land that is made up of rubber" and also called its inhabitants Olmecs which translates to "rubber inhabitants."

The Olmec territory, as you can will see, was filled with Panama rubber trees and the trade in rubber was a major element of the cultural. The Olmecs in common together with Aztecs and Maya were also fond of throwing around with a rubber ball and some have even pointed out that the famous Olmec stone heads appear like they're wearing helmets for football made of rubber. Did this explain why they were referred to as the people who wore rubber? Because they wore headgear made of rubber?

In any case, the Olmecs were located on the Mexican Gulf Coast, and their culture lasted from 1500 to around 400 BC. The most preserved Olmec settlements can be seen in the present-day cities of San Lorenzo and La Venta, Mexico. Olmec architects were adept in carving out stone structures and working Aqueducts. They also built one of the oldest-known pyramids within the Americas. The structures that stand out most are the striking stone heads that are scattered across their towns.

The heads, which appear to be wearing some kind of unusual helmet look out with a serious and stoic face. Within one complex that consists of a ceremonial step-pyramid with a few smaller buildings around it, there are massive stone heads looking out across the entire length of the building. What was the significance of these statues? Did they serve as guards looking out for dangers?

The most plausible theory is that the Olmecs served some kind of religious significance. In many ways the stones of the Olmecs are identical to the ones found in Easter Island, and the Easter Islanders worshiped their moai that they came to believe were incarnations of spirits of their deceased ancestral ancestors. Are the Olmecs believed to have had similar beliefs?

The Olmecs had an extensive, intricate religion, but all that we have learned about them has to be derived from their art and artifacts, as the Olmec writings have not been identified. There is evidence that suggests that the Olmecs had a priestly group that governed the congregation. We also are aware that they worshipped a variety of gods, many of whom were half-human, and half animal in their the natural world. One appeared to be half manand one half jaguar, and the other was known as the "sky-dragon."

One of the Olmecs' most stunning sculptures -- and one that has garnered some attention is the"so-called "ancient astronaut in the control." This is a picture of an old Olmec sitting in what appears like a cockpit, his hands operating levers and dials. Of course, it might be the way some think through their current lens of knowledge, however In reality, the artifact may not have anything to anything to do with space travel. It could be a type of religious symbolism we're not yet able to comprehend.

In addition to being top-quality sculpturers the Olmecs were excellent traders. Their trade networks included a variety of outposts, which helped in the movement of goods across Mesoamerica. The Olmecs traded their artifacts and rubber , and imported jade designs, jewelry made of obsidian, as well as numerous other products all over the world. It is this commercial activity that has been used to chart the various stages of their decline. At first, in the San Lorenzo settlement began to decline, with the majority of the trade shifting into La Venta. As time passed it was decided that the La Venta site was abandoned too. What did the Olmecs do?

Many believe they would die if they were unable to expand their diet. Archaeological digs have proved they were picky eaters, whose meals revolved mostly on sweet potato, squash as well as maize (corn). As environmental pressures caused it to be more difficult to grow these food crops and the Olmecs began to decline.

If you believe this to sound like an unimaginably simple explanation for why the great civilization fell to pieces, you're not alone and a variety of alternatives have been proposed. One theory may be the fact that the Olmecs were defeated in the war against one of their adversaries. Another theory is that the environmental change created a lot of silt in the local rivers which in turn reduced supply of water. Whatever the reason that quiet stone sentries they left behind inspire us to think.

Finding the Riddle of Angkor Wat

Angkor Wat is a temple complex which is located in the present-day Southeast Asian nation of Cambodia. The temple complex is situated in Angkor which was the capital in Khmer Empire. Khmer Empire. In the 9th century, the Khmer had created the kingdom that later became an imposing family. The kings of the Khmer were called "varman" which was clever and powerful Suryay-varman II that built Angkor Wat.

The name translates to "Temple City" It is actually a large complex of temples and sacred artifacts. The Khmer were fervent Hindus during the time of the building of Angkor Wat as well. Temple City is a grand symbol of their religion. The three great spires on The main structure are thought to be the mountains of the future and the moat that surrounds the temple reflects the forever-lasting waters of the creation.

The most commonly held misconception concerning Hinduism can be that it's a multitheistic faith. But, Hinduism is actually "henotheistic." This is a type of monotheism, which argues that, even though there is one God and the ultimate god is too vast for us human beings to comprehend. Therefore, the divine force helps us out a little through its manifestation in array of ways. The renowned 330,000 gods in Hinduism are, in essence, the numerous manifestations of the one supreme being. The supreme being, who seems to remain largely inaccessible from both time and space is known as Brahma. Brahma's lesser forms like Vishnu as the "preserver for life" as well as Shiva who is the "destroyer and destroyer of the universe" that are working within the universe. Angkor Wat was built to demonstrate these complex belief systems through the architecture of the temple as well as the carvings that are there.

The principal rival of the Khmer Empire is the Champa Kingdom located in what is now the southern part of Vietnam. There was a constant conflict between the Khmer and Champa were constantly fighting over resources and territory The aspect that Champa were Buddhists was a further source of tension. It's not to say that there weren't Buddhists within the Khmer Empire, but nonetheless the issue of religious animosity was a major factor in the war between these two kingdoms.

The battle came to an end in 1177 AD, when the Champa succeeded in capturing in 1177 AD the Khmer Empire and broke into Angkor Wat itself. They were later exiled however the fact that the temple complex was burned to the ground seems to have hit a nerve with Khmer people. A few began to doubt their faith, asking "Why did Vishnu come to our rescue?"

After this disaster after the incident, an entirely new Khmer leader named Jaya-varman VII was elected to the top position. And it is a Buddhist. Jaya-varman VII changed the face of Angkor Wat by rededicating it to Buddhism. It may seem odd to the Khmer to suddenly embrace that religion as their foes However, after all that they had gone through, they thought, "Well if you can't beat them, join em'!" In any case, as it was a significant shift it could seem, people generally accepted the changes and, soon enough, the primary religious practice in Khmer people was Khmer Empire became Buddhism instead of Hinduism.

After its shift to the Buddhist religion, Angkor Wat reached another peak during the 1400s but then began a slow decline. The people who worshipped in the temple complex gradually reducing their attendance and rumours were circulating that the temple's grounds were cursed by evil spirits. Then, only a handful of monks were left to manage the massive temple grounds. At the time Europeans came across the area during the sixteenth century it was almost abandoned and dense jungle vegetation was poised to take over the entire complex.

The next person from outside to arrive at Angkor Wat was a French researcher called Henri Mouhot, who came to the site in 1859. In 1860, it is Mouhot that popularized the idea of The Temple City was built by an ancient civilization. However, in reality the civilization that constructed the temple wasn't gone. In fact, the Khmer inhabitants were in the area but they had abandoned the work their ancestors had built.

The Mysterious Maya

The Maya have captivated archaeologists and scholars since their cities, which were abandoned, came to light in the late 19th century. However, the story of the Maya people started thousands of years earlier was even discovered. In fact, they never really stopped. About six million Maya reside in the southeastern regions of Mexico, Guatemala, Honduras as well as El Salvador to this very day. They use old Mayan language that is traced back to mysterious ancestral ancestors.

Even the contemporary Maya could not explain the reason why these great cities were abandoned and buried in the trees and overgrown vegetation. True that Spanish colonists made contacts with some of the final vestiges from the Maya civilisation and spent the next few hundred years eradicating the remaining tribes between 1527 until 1697. The actual essence that was the Maya civilization has, however, vanished prior to the time that Europeans came to the area.

The Maya's origins in the region date back to approximately 2600 BC. The earliest settlements of this time are located within the Mexican Yucatan Peninsula. The Maya in the early days weren't yet a huge empire, and they'd benefit from the cultures that were before them, like the Olmecs, when they started to build their own grand civilization.

The archaeological evidence suggests that the Maya came in their own and become a mighty civilization around 200 AD. Around this time in the known as Maya lowlands in the Maya lowlands, that they constructed some of their first significant stone monuments , and then began to develop urban zones around the monuments. They developed into complicated cities that were interconnected to each other until they created their own Maya Empire. In the 4th century, at the end of the century Teotihuacan was the strongest of Maya cities, and was able to conquer the others, and thus began an era known as the Teotihuacan Dynasty.

It's real the fact that Teotihuacan has an Aztec name, but even though the Aztecs eventually conquered the city the city, it was established through the Maya. Other noteworthy Maya cities included Palenque, Rio Bec, Tikal, Copan, Calakmul and Uaxactuc. Each of these cities had populations of at least 50,000 and they all shared the same construction plans with the communal plazas, palaces ball courts, and temples (where the Maya struck the ball with a rubber) were regular fixtures. The cities were surrounded by huge farms, where the poorer class worked to produce enough food to sustain the all of the inhabitants.

It was true that equality wasn't necessarily a norm within Maya society. Within their order of things there was the kuhul ajaw , or "holy Lords" who controlled the day. The holy lords claimed that they be descended from gods and were guided by a family-based type of divine right. Kuhul Ajaws were the direct intermediaries between mankind and the celestial beings that the Maya were revered.

In addition to improving their statecraft, social structure and beliefs in religion The Maya also made remarkable advancements in math and astronomy. They were the first to discover the concept of zero without distinction from the majority of humanity. They also created accurate calendars for marking both the all-year-round calendar and their famous "long count" that counts the days five thousand years ahead.

This was actually the Maya Long Count Calendar that generated the rage in 2012 due to the fact that it's "13th b'ak'tun" was completed on the 21st day of December the year. It was just a way to mark the passage of the passage of time for the Maya however, even though many others have repeatedly suggested that the closing on the 13th of December might be the cause of massive, apocalyptic turmoil however, the Maya did not really suggest the idea. It was the ending of an era, however, it was it was not the end of the world.

But it is true that the Maya had also utilized their expertise in astronomy to predict accurately that a planetary alignment could take place at the winter solstice on December 21 2012. Some conspiracy theorists seized on this information to argue that the motion of celestial bodies in alignment might spell our demise with a flurry of cataclysms, including shifts in polarity and such. As this is writing in the beginning of 2020s, none of that has ever occurred.

The Maya continued to develop as a major civilization in Mesoamerica and reached their highest level by the year 1000 AD. They would be in a position of absolute dominance over the region, prosperity and peace up to the 1400s. In the 1400s, unrest started to develop within Maya society. Although it's not known the root of this conflict and the Maya began to abandon some of their major cities.

At the time that Spanish conquistadors came down to Yucatan in the late 1800s, the Maya were barely a shadow of their glory of the past. They held on to only some key cities with their capital cities and enormous pyramid temples abandoned. The Spaniards initially believed that they believed that the Maya were wiped out by a different indigenous group. This theory, however, does not make sense due to various reasons.

First , the Maya are at highest level at the time. There was no other group from Mesoamerica could have been able to pose this kind of threat. In addition, even if other people could have pushed them out of them but there is no evidence that a war was ever fought. The cities they once inhabited are not showing any war damage, and they appear like they were abandoned prior to the centuries of plant growth swept them away.

Another popular idea lately suggests that Maya was hit by a severe drought, a one that was so severe that people just walked away in search of a place with better water access. It's possible, but it is a rather extreme reaction to completely leave entire cityscapes behind since this is not in a desert and therefore it is likely that some water remained.

Another hypothesis, which has gained a certain luster from the time of the COVID-19 epidemic, suggests that Maya were struck by a horrible illness. It is possible that a deadly plague killed the vast majority of people, and then left survivors running in fear that they were infected too. However, this is a plausible explanation for the Maya leaving entire cities. In the meantime that the Black Death was killing huge number of people across Europe, yet European cities were not completely removed from the population.

With no clear reason to explain this sudden abandonment there are many conspiracy theories that have been developed in regards towards the Maya. The most well-known theories is based on is the Ancient Astronaut theory, which claims that many ancient civilizations had visitors from the stars. For those who support the theory of Ancient Astronauts, it's simple to claim that an technologically advanced species flew down and took the residents of these crowded Maya cities to...well someplace else!

However, is there any evidence to support such assertions? No However, if we extend our imagination, we can find several archaeological sources that could be used to suggest it is possible that people of the Maya had contact with ETs and were even instructed in flying their spacecraft.

Their belief system speaks of connection with the heavenly realms, and in particular, the "feathered serpent" who was able to impart great knowledge to them. Legends of theirs also foretell the day that these celestial beings would return to Earth and bring them back. Ancient scientists believe that the heavenly beings are extraterrestrials that did come back to retrieve Maya Maya up in their spacecrafts. It's as simple as that and all of the Maya towns were abandoned due to the fact that their inhabitants were given a one-way clock that took them to another world.

To prove this ancient astronaut theorists refer to an odd artifact that is particularly notable -- the famous top of the tombstone of King Pakal which was discovered within Palenque. Maya area of Palenque. The lid of the sarcophagus that Pakal was buried in shows the dead king frantically operating the controls in what is believed to be the cockpit of an spacecraft. The person who started the whole craze of ancient astronauts, Erich von Daniken, stated it as follows:

"There is a human and the top of his body bending forward like a racer Today, any child can think of his vehicle as rockets. It's pointed towards the front, changes to oddly grooved indentations that resemble ports for inlet, expands to the tail with a flaming flame. The person crouching is manipulating several indefinable controls . He also has an ankle of his left mounted on the pedal."

It is the most accurate description of the work the King Pakal performs in this sculpture. The king is bent inwards, and appears to be operating controls using his hands, while his feet are working an electric pedal below. It is true that one could see the compartment's bottom below in which Pakal is sitting as flames bursting out.

It could be just what our current ideas inform us. The Maya were known to be a lover of abstract art and the imagination of a sculptor just went off with him. However until we find other artifacts, or find the forgotten Maya writings that might provide us with additional clues, the jury will be out about what really transpired to the mysterious civilization of the Maya.

The Lost Viking Colonies

In in the eighth century longships left from Nordic ports to embark on an extended journey into the vast unknown. These ships were led by fierce warriors and seafarers referred to as Vikings However, exactly what they were seeking isn't quite certain. Maybe they were looking seeking a new spot to rest their heads, or an exciting new epic (great tale) to be told. However, whatever brought them out into the sea pushed them to remote locations like Iceland or Greenland.

The Vikings were master navigators and these were amazing feats of exploration in the era. However, for centuries these maritime feats were masked by the Vikings notorious practice of dropping down on unaware Europeans as well as setting towns and churches in flames. True it's true that the Vikings have been long known for their zeal for war than their achievements. While it's not necessarily wrong but this part from Viking historical record has been altered and altered by people who have been responsible for the telling.

It's true that Vikings were brutal and cruel when they arrived in countries such as Britain or set monasteries on fire. However, in their minds they were fighting the holy battle to Christian Europe. It is true that these Viking attacks began as a reaction against the Catholic church's attempts to bring Vikings into Christianity. Charlemagne had sent troops to convert Vikings in regions like Saxony and Denmark and at one point , he ordered his troops to burn an ancient tree believed to be considered sacred to Norse.

For the Vikings it was not just an unforgivable, sacrilegious crime. They literally sparked Armageddon. This tree is a symbol of Yggdrasil which is which is the life-giving tree in Norse mythology. According to ancient prophecies that if the tree of old were destroyed Ragnarok will descend. This caused the Vikings in a rage, and shortly following, they launched an all-out battle against Europe.

A year later, after Charlemagne ordered destroyed the Norse altar in Saxony destroyed in 773 AD, the Vikings began to attack England. A series of skirmishes culminated into an eerie attack on the 16th of June, 793. A Viking group of raiders destroyed the Christian monastery located on the island of Lindisfarne and killed anyone who was near. The hysterical attacks continued for the next century, and by the time 900 AD at the time, the Vikings had sacked every important European nation.

As fierce and ruthless as Vikings were,, Christian Europe was much more organized and populated It was that it was only a matter until the Vikings had to switch to Christianity. It is interesting to note that while the brutal war was going on in the west, this Viking management was sending its finest ships and explorers to west in search of a new territories. Are the Vikings truly seeking a new home, in which they could live in liberty from Christians? Certainly, they were.

A few of the more well-known Vikings such as Erik the Red --is believed to leave Iceland in the year 1000 AD shortly following the Althing (a type that was a kind of Norse parliament) decided to contemplate converting to Christianity. In the case of Erik the Red an avid follower of the Norse religion it was a travesty and he decided to embarked on a voyage to Greenland.

However, Vikings such as Erik the Red might not have just been looking for a spot to escape to; they may be looking to find Valhalla itself. In the same way that Valhalla represented a sort of heaven for Vikings According to Viking legend, there was a real physical location, a homeland that was believed to lie in West of Scandinavia. Did

Vikings looking for their lost homeland when they accidentally came across an American continent? The motivation to locate it would surely have been impressive, considering that according to the legend those who discovered Valhalla would be immediately gifted the promise of eternal life.

The first person to do so is Erik The Red's son Leif Erikson, thought to be among the first European to step foot on the northernmost tip of the North American continent. Leif Erikson had gotten to the area through a narrative written by a former Norse explorator, Bjarni Herjolfsson, who had been lost in the sea while en route towards Greenland during 986 AD. Bjarni said that she had glimpsed the shores of a mysterious continent prior to his ability to turn around his ship. After this information, Leif Erikson confirmed that the far western continent did exist. The area was awash in wild grapes Leif called the land Vinland (Wine Land). Leif and his crew embarked on their boats and built shelters along the coast which they stayed in for the winter. As spring rolled in and they returned to their boats and headed back home.

A few years later but Leif Erikson's older brother Thorvald set off in an effort to follow Leif's footsteps. Leif's expedition did not make any contact with local inhabitants throughout their stay on America's northeast coast and they were aware, the continent was not inhabited. However, it was certainly not. Thorvald's encounter for the first time with Native Americans was not very enjoyable. After a heated exchange that ended in death, Thorvald was struck by an arrow struck his side. The survivors laid him to rest in the North American continent and then returned to Greenland to tell their terrifying story.

The death of Thorvald's did not deter the next adventurers. A few years after the Norse merchant called Thorfinn Karlsefni, along with his wife, who was pregnant Gudrid as well as 65 other colonists, returned to the steps of Thorvald's tragically lost journey and headed for the northern shores of America. In this area, Gurdid was the mother of Snorri who was the first child of the explorers born in this mysterious new country. The initial situation was tranquil, but once the warm weather of spring began to arrive and the Vikings began to become aware of the indigenous Native Americans. Thorfinn's initial exchanges group engaged in with the locals were more constructive. There was not any fighting or bloodshed. In reality they started trading products, most notably furs.

Although they Native Americans were happy to purchase furs, they appeared to be more interested in Vikings with their swords and axes. Thorfinn advised his soldiers not to trade them in the event that they would later be employed against them. But this opposition to trading weapons may have sparked some anger. And during the summer, some residents tried to seize certain of the Vikings weapons by force. The incident resulted in deaths of several Native Americans, which then resulted in a retaliatory attack against an Viking settlement. They Vikings could stop the attack by their sheer force.

According to legend that according to legend, it was Leif Erikson's half-sister in law Freydis Eirksdottir that was able to scare their enemies more than any other. Freydis is said to have shouted so loudly in a rage of anger when she was wielding her sword she scared all those who were around her. Screams that sounded bloody aside, however the Vikings recognized that even though they were outnumbered in the long run, their chances of survival were slim. In the following spring the Vikings returned to Greenland.

The brave Freydis herself who commanded the next expedition, and landed again after a few years. However, this time, the Viking colony soon broke up not because of external tension but because of internal conflict The Vikings began to fight in such a way that they made the decision to end their squabble and return home.

The only trip to America that is recorded in the Viking epics is Erik Gnupson, who set sail in 1121 AD. After that, little else is recorded about Erik Gnupson or his crew. What did they do to these Viking explorationists? Did they get lost at the sea? Perhaps they established the undiscovered Viking settlement in America?

As they weren't able to send an email or snail mail to update their followers It could be possible that they simply moved to the American coast and did not return. It's interesting to note that in 1961, archaeologists discovered a whole colony that consisted of Viking Longhouses found in Newfoundland. It was confirmed that it was an actual Viking settlement after they discovered iron tools. Native Americans at that time didn't have iron but the Vikings certainly had iron. Archaeologists also discovered an iron spindle that would be utilized to Viking women to create clothes.

However, Newfoundland is colder than Vinland which is cold enough for the grapes that were grown throughout Vinland in such great abundance. Therefore, it is likely to be that Newfoundland settlement happened to be one the Viking stories did not mention in their sagas. Could this be the place where Erik Gnupson ended up and created his own self-governing Viking colony? Perhaps we'll never know.

Conclusion

With the inherent human desire to explore and discover and discovery, we learn not just our own lives, but also the environment around us and the way in which history was created by nature, different cultures, through wars, and through the fusion of cultures. What we learn from the lost cities and civilizations the world over are a few of the forgotten pieces of our collective history as inhabitants of the planet. We can gain insight into the skills and creativity of our ancestors by studying historical relics and the remnants of a previous time , and we can better connect and comprehend our fellow human beings when we understand that we all are part of a living culture which is built on the past and is alive in the present , and optimistic towards the future.

As time passes the more ancient civilizations and lost sites will be found to be discovered, examined and studied. It's an extremely fascinating thing as each new discovery adds to our culture.

I would like to express my gratitude for taking the time to read this book and I hope it has provided you with some idea, however short of how the world's civilizations have evolved and, in a few cases reversed, how we all fit into global society, all of us a descendant of civilizations and cultures that were able to comprehend the wonders that we see through archaeology and the past architectural and artistic works as well as exploration and tradition.

CPSIA information can be obtained
at www.ICGtesting.com
Printed in the USA
BVHW052246090223
658263BV00007B/223